Education for Tomorrow's Jobs

Susan W. Sherman, *Editor*

Committee on Vocational Education and
Economic Development in Depressed Areas

Commission on Behavioral and Social Sciences
and Education

National Research Council

NATIONAL ACADEMY PRESS
Washington, D.C.   1983

National Academy Press, 2101 Constitution Avenue, NW, Washington, DC 20418

NOTICE: The project that is the subject of this report was approved by the Governing Board of the National Research Council, whose members are drawn from the councils of the National Academy of Sciences, the National Academy of Engineering, and the Institute of Medicine. The members of the committee responsible for the report were chosen for their special competences and with regard for appropriate balance.

This report has been reviewed by a group other than the authors according to procedures approved by a Report Review Committee consisting of members of the National Academy of Sciences, the National Academy of Engineering, and the Institute of Medicine.

The National Research Council was established by the National Academy of Sciences in 1916 to associate the broad community of science and technology with the Academy's purposes of furthering knowledge and of advising the federal government. The Council operates in accordance with general policies determined by the Academy under the authority of its congressional charter of 1863, which establishes the Academy as a private, nonprofit, self-governing membership corporation. The Council has become the principal operating agency of both the National Academy of Sciences and the National Academy of Engineering in the conduct of their services to the government, the public, and the scientific and engineering communities. It is administered jointly by both Academies and the Institute of Medicine. The National Academy of Engineering and the Institute of Medicine were established in 1964 and 1970, respectively, under the charter of the National Academy of Sciences.

This project has been funded with funds from the U.S. Department of Education under contract number 300-81-0306. The contents of this publication do not necessarily reflect the views or policies of the U.S. Department of Education nor does mention of trade names, commercial products, or organizations imply endorsement by the U.S. government.

Library of Congress Cataloging Publication Data

National Research Council (U.S.). Committee on Vocational Education and Economic Development in Depressed Areas.
    Education for tomorrow's jobs.

    Bibliography: p.
    Includes index.
    1. Socially handicapped youth — Education — United States. 2. Vocational education — Economic aspects — United States. 3. Socially handicapped youth — Employment — United States. 4. Industry and education — Economic aspects — United States. I. Sherman, Susan W.
    II. Title.
    LC4091.N367   1983   370.19'31   83-17304
    ISBN 0-309-03392-6

First Printing, September 1983
Second Printing, April 1984
Third Printing, August 1984

Printed in the United States of America

iii

Preface

The Committee on Vocational Education and Economic Development in Depressed Areas was established at the request of the U.S. Department of Education in October 1981. This request reflected the general public concern over the country's deteriorating economic condition, particularly unemployment and inflation. The charge from the department to the committee was "to undertake a study of collaborative efforts among business, industry, and community-based organizations and the public sector in the vocational education of residents, particularly minority residents, of economically depressed areas." We were urged at our first meeting by the Under Secretary of Education and the Assistant Secretary for Vocational and Adult Education to bring a new perspective to the relationships among vocational education, economic development, and the private sector.

When this committee began its deliberations, unemployment among older teenagers was more than 23 percent and unemployment among black teenagers was approaching a staggering 48 percent. At the same time, the weaknesses in our economy and fundamental changes in the patterns of American employment were having a profound impact on older workers, such that overall unemployment was reaching the highest levels since the Great Depression. It was in this environment that we began our study of vocational education, which is the part of the education enterprise that deals most directly with the ties between work and learning and which should hold out significant hope for education to have a long-term impact on the opportunities of young Americans throughout their careers.

Within the broad mandate that we received, the committee identified and addressed those problems that we saw to be of the most pressing and immediate concern. In particular, we focused on how vocational education, in collaboration with private-sector employers, can improve the employability of young Americans and enhance their long-term contributions to the economy. In doing so the committee chose to examine the role of vocational education in overall economic development and did not restrict itself exclusively to issues associated with vocational education in depressed areas. We believe that the challenges and opportunities facing vocational education are not unique to depressed areas, although the severity of the problems that must be overcome is certainly exacerbated by weak economic conditions.

We also chose to direct our analysis and recommendations to the education and training of young people who are just embarking on their employment careers. This emphasis reflects the importance that the committee placed on the attainment of basic employment and learning skills that are necessary for successful participation in a continually changing economy. The committee considered the important issues concerning the retraining of older workers displaced by the changing economy but decided that the problems of these workers were sufficiently different as to require separate study.

Just as the committee began its deliberations in an atmosphere of concern about the national economy, we are now completing our work in an atmosphere of concern about the state of the American education system. This report focuses on that part of the education system that deals most directly with the lifetime relationship between learning and work. The current circumstances provide an opportunity for actions to be taken that can have fundamental and long-term effects on the education system. It is in this setting that we put forward the analysis and recommendations contained in this report.

COLIN C. BLAYDON, *Chair*
Committee on Vocational Education and
Economic Development in Depressed
Areas

Acknowledgments

A number of people have contributed significantly to our work. In addition to the expertise and knowledge brought to our discussions by the individual committee members, we also convened workshops with outside participation and commissioned two papers. We wish to thank John Bishop, Henry David, Richard Elmore, Becky Hayward, Gerry Hendrickson, Charles Mallar, Elizabeth Reisner, and Sean Sullivan for their presentations and participation in our workshop discussions. Two committee members, Paul Peterson and Charles Benson, also made valuable presentations of their work at one of the workshops. In addition, the committee is indebted to the authors of the two papers: Michael E. Borus, author of "A Descriptive Analysis of Employed and Unemployed Youth," and Sean Sullivan, author of "Private Initiatives to Improve Youth Employment." Their work provided valuable assistance to the development of this report.

One person who was not a member of the committee contributed generously of his time and expertise. Charles Cooke, a colleague of committee member Wilson Riles, participated actively in the committee's deliberations and provided valuable information for the report. He deserves our special thanks.

We wish to thank Robert M. Worthington, Assistant Secretary for Vocational and Adult Education, and his staff at the U.S. Department of Education for their support and assistance as sponsors of this project. Glenn Boerrigter, Doris Gunderson, Howard F. Hjelm, Jack A. Wilson, and Steven Zwillinger all deserve our appreciation.

Susan W. Sherman served as study director for this project from its inception. Her skillful organization of the research effort gave substance to our deliberations, and she bore the responsibility for writing successive drafts of this report with tact and good judgment.

We owe our thanks, too, to other members of the National Research Council staff. Barbara A. Malone served as administrative secretary to the committee, thoughtfully arranging the details of our meetings and providing secretarial support. José R. Dizon capably assisted in the preparation of the final manuscript. Heidi I. Hartmann, associate executive director of the Commission on Behavioral and Social Sciences and Education, provided valuable substantive advice early in the project. Alexandra K. Wigdor, study director of the Committee on the Performance of Military Personnel, was generous with her guidance and intellectual support of our efforts. David A. Goslin, executive director of the commission, and Eugenia Grohman, associate director for reports of the commission, read drafts of the report and made valuable substantive and organizational suggestions. Christine L. McShane, editor of the commission, in editing the report made significant contributions in matters of substance as well as style.

Finally, I wish to thank the members of the committee for their candor, their equanimity, and their hard work.

COLIN C. BLAYDON

Contents

Education for Tomorrow's Jobs

Summary

Unemployment among young people is a serious and persistent problem in this country. Unemployment rates are especially high among members of minority groups, for high-school dropouts, and in economically depressed areas. The structural changes in the economy in the past 40 years have far-reaching implications for the skills that young workers will need and for the education and training that will increase their employability. Vocational education and other training programs can help to alleviate the problem of unemployment among America's young people. And a close link between schools and employers can help ensure that vocational education programs are teaching students the skills that employers will need.

Vocational education is a vital part of the public education system in this country, one that has long been slighted in favor of academic education. Basic academic as well as occupational skills are of fundamental importance in preparing young people for productive lives in our society. The public elementary and secondary schools in this country should offer students who will not go to college a thorough grounding not only in language skills, reasoning, and mathematics, but also in the mechanical and technical skills and work habits that will prepare them for working life. This responsibility should not be shifted to private-sector employers, although employers can help significantly in ways we outline in the report.

Evaluations of vocational education and other employment training programs lead to the conclusion that some vocational education programs do improve the employability of graduates. But the quality of vocational education programs overall is highly variable and the access of dis-

1

advantaged students to good programs is not ensured.

The committee recommends expanded collaboration between vocational educators and private-sector employers as well as improved coordination between vocational education and employment training programs. Well-designed work experience programs help to improve occupational skills and to open employment opportunities for vocational education students. We recommend several changes intended to strengthen the capabilities of teachers of vocational education: changes in certification requirements, pre-service and in-service training, use of part-time teachers, and pay scales of teachers. We recommend three policy changes to improve the financing of vocational education programs: modifications in the formulas for funding programs, strategies for pooling equipment, and supplementary funding for program improvement. Because of our concern about the limited access of disadvantaged students to high-quality programs, we also recommend experimentation with vocational incentive grants to individual students, which they could use to purchase the training they desire, and attention to consumer protection in vocational education programs.

1 *Youth Unemployment in a Changing Economy*

Overview

Unemployment among young Americans is currently a serious and complex problem. Some of the nearly 3 million people ages 16-21 who could not find full-time or part-time jobs in 1982 are victims of the ailing U.S. economy. Presumably some of them will be able to get and hold jobs once the current recession has eased. Some of them are simply engaged in looking for jobs and will find them in time. Others may be the victims of various social conditions—structural changes in the economy; lingering discrimination on the basis of racial or ethnic background, gender, or age; or an education system that has not kept pace with technological change or has not taught all students basic educational or occupational skills. These latter young people, many of whom are high-school dropouts, are unemployed—and perhaps unemployable—because they lack the basic skills, the occupational skills, or the attitudes necessary in the workplace. They represent a major failing of the education system, even though some may have passed "successfully" through that system. It is this system, in particular vocational education in the public high schools, that is the focus of this report.

Our goal in this report is to recommend ways in which the education system, particularly the public vocational education system, can be improved in order to enhance the employability of its graduates. We recommend strengthening the ties between vocational education and employers as a means of improving vocational education programs. We outline institutional changes that will be required of the vocational education system before effective collaborative efforts with business and industry can be made. We believe also that education and training constitute a lifelong

3

endeavor to keep every person's knowledge and skills up-to-date and that education and employment policies should be made consistent with that view. Because of the rapid rate of technological change in our society, it is no longer practical or feasible to consider that people receive all the training they will need throughout their careers while they are young and in school.

We begin by presenting the economic context of the study. In this first chapter we discuss structural changes in the U.S. economy, changes in the nature of jobs, and changes in the skills required in jobs that affect people's employment prospects. We then narrow the scope of the discussion to youth unemployment, describing its nature and extent and putting it in the context of national economic conditions. We highlight the education implications of these different types of employment conditions. We try to portray the complexity and severity of the problem by examining employment experiences for different groups of young people, their educational backgrounds, the types of work they are seeking, and other relevant social factors. Clearly, unemployment has vastly different meanings for different groups of young people. For example, a 17-year-old high-school student living with his or her middle-class parents may be looking for a part-time job principally to earn extra spending money. In contrast, unemployment would have much more serious implications for a 19-year-old male high-school dropout trying to support his family and himself or for a 20-year-old divorced mother trying to support her child and herself.

We go on to describe the current vocational education system in Chapter 2, highlighting the diversity of offerings and the variable quality of its programs. We describe the institutional and administrative arrangements typical of vocational education programs. Working from recent evaluative studies, we describe those programs that tend to expand and improve the education and employment prospects of their graduates. We observe that good vocational education programs are often distinguished by their close ties with business, a theme that is developed more fully in Chapter 3. We also analyze problems relating to limited access to high-quality programs available to the students most in need of education and employment opportunities.

In Chapter 3 we discuss collaborative ventures involving vocational education, private-sector employers, labor unions, and community-based organizations. Collaboration is not a novel idea; such efforts have been made for years, but they could be expanded considerably to improve the education and the employability of the students. We outline some economic development strategies involving education and training that are intended to accommodate technological changes and restore health to the economies of depressed areas. Such strategies are characterized by collaboration between vocational education programs and private-sector employers.

The committee then presents its conclusions regarding the strengths and weaknesses of the vocational education system and its diverse programs in Chapter 4. We present our argument for using an improved system of vocational education as an available, practical, and effective means of combating the employment problems of many American young people. We present recommendations for strengthening vocational education so that it, in turn, can help young Americans and, ultimately, the economy. We argue that links between school and work should be strengthened because they will help improve the quality and increase the relevance of the training that vocational education students receive. We describe features of the many forms of collaborative efforts that appear to be necessary for success, and we outline measures designed to reduce rigidities within the vocational education system so that collaborative efforts can occur without impediment. We emphasize our belief in the value of supervised work experience for vocational education students by describing the important features of beneficial arrangements, recommending expanded opportunities for students to work, and recommending some modifications in work experience programs.

We present two sets of recommendations for improving vocational education, especially in high schools. The first concerns teachers—their certification, their training (both pre-service and in-service), their pay scales, and the use of part-time teachers. The second deals with the financing of vocational education—funding formulas, pooling equipment, and funding for program improvement. We conclude by suggesting experimental approaches to improve the access of disadvantaged students to high-quality vocational education programs.

STRUCTURAL CHANGES IN THE ECONOMY

Fundamental changes in the American economy over the last 40 years—in the types of goods manufactured here, in the ways in which those goods are produced, in the types of services that are rendered, in the balance between the manufacturing and service sectors, in the position of the United States in the world economy, and in the responses of the private sector to technological innovation—have had dramatic effects on the nature of jobs. Many education and training programs have not kept pace with these structural changes and with technological advances affecting large numbers of occupations.

The Shift from Manufacturing to Service Jobs

Discussion about unemployment currently turns rather quickly to the topic of changes in the types of jobs in the American economy—the widely

discussed shift from manufacturing to service jobs. Manufacturing is generally taken to include the production of goods (everything from paper clips,
bakery goods, and automobiles to industrial equipment) as well as the
processing of materials (petroleum products, metals, plastics, and chemi-
cals, for example). The service sector includes such a diversity of jobs that
some economists discourage grouping them together under the term *service
sector* because of its illusion of uniformity (see Stanback et al., 1981). One
classification scheme, used by the Committee on National Urban Policy
(Hanson, 1983), divides the service sector into the following categories:
distributive services, the complex of corporate activities and producer
services (such as finance, insurance, real estate), nonprofit services (health
and education), retail services, consumer services (for example, hotels,
auto repair, amusements), and government and government enterprises.
Furthermore, as we shall see, not all jobs in the manufacturing sector are
directly involved in the production process; some of them are very similar to
jobs in the service sector.

The proportion of jobs in the manufacturing sector has been declining
since the end of World War II, while the proportion in the service sector has
been increasing (Table 1). In 1940, 34 percent of nonagricultural workers
were engaged in manufacturing. This proportion decreased to 22 percent in
1980. Between 1940 and 1980 employment in the service sector rose from
59 percent to 72 percent of all those employed outside agriculture. From
Table 1 we can calculate that approximately 84 percent of all new jobs
introduced into the economy between 1940 and 1980 were in the service
sector.

Changes in union membership over time give further testimony to these
economic shifts. The National Commission for Employment Policy (1982)
noted that in 1960 the United Auto Workers and the United Steelworkers of
America were the two largest unions in the AFL-CIO. By 1980 the two
largest unions were the United Food and Commercial Workers and the
American Federation of State, County, and Municipal Employees.

Compared with the period before World War II, manufacturing industries currently employ proportionately fewer workers to actually make
products, while more workers are involved in invention, design, management, and sales. And the changes continue, many say at an accelerating
rate. Some jobs currently filled by workers will be performed by robots, and
other jobs will involve working with the robots. An increasing proportion of
manufacturing jobs require some education or training, and there are fewer
jobs for low-skilled manual laborers (Hanson, 1983). Some jobs now
require more knowledge, while others are being broken into discrete,
routine components that require little thought and even less imagination.

TABLE 1   Percentage Distribution of Employees on Nonagricultural
Payrolls, by Industry Division, 1940-1980

Industry Division	1940	1950	1960	1970	1980
Total	100	100	100	100	100
	(32,361)	(45,197)	(54,189)	(70,880)	(90,406)
Goods-producing	41	41	37	33	28
	(13,221)	(18,506)	(20,434)	(23,578)	(25,658)
Mining	3	2	1	1	1
	(925)	(901)	(712)	(623)	(1,027)
Construction	4	5	5	5	5
	(1,311)	(2,364)	(2,926)	(3,588)	(4,346)
Manufacturing	34	34	31	27	22
	(10,985)	(15,241)	(16,796)	(19,367)	(20,285)
Service-producing	59	59	62	67	72
	(19,140)	(26,691)	(33,755)	(47,302)	(67,748)
Transportation and public utilities	9	9	7	6	6
	(3,038)	(4,034)	(4,004)	(4,515)	(5,146)
Wholesale and retail trade	21	21	21	21	22
	(6,750)	(9,386)	(11,391)	(14,040)	(20,310)
Finance, insurance, real estate	5	4	5	5	6
	(1,485)	(1,888)	(2,629)	(3,645)	(5,160)
Services	11	12	14	16	20
	(3,665)	(5,357)	(7,378)	(11,548)	(17,890)
Government	13	13	15	18	18
	(4,202)	(6,026)	(8,353)	(12,554)	(16,241)
Federal	3	4	4	4	3
	(996)	(1,928)	(2,270)	(2,731)	(2,866)
State and local	10	9	11	14	15
	(3,206)	(4,098)	(6,083)	(9,823)	(13,375)

NOTE: Numbers in parentheses represent thousands.

SOURCE: Bureau of Labor Statistics, 1983, *Employment and Earnings* 30(3) March:
Table B-1.

There is diversity and change in the service sector as well. Some jobs
require considerable knowledge or education, but others do not. The more
knowledge-intensive jobs, having higher status, offer good incomes and
opportunities for advancement. Stanback et al. (1981) present an analysis of

data from the 1970 census showing that in general those employed in service jobs have higher education levels than those working in manufacturing (Table 2). Of course in some service jobs, such as cleaning and maintenance of dwellings and other buildings, education levels are roughly the same as or lower than levels in manufacturing jobs. They conclude that most young people today enter the labor market through jobs in retailing and consumer services rather than through jobs in farming or manufacturing, as they did before World War II. Since these service jobs generally require more education than those in manufacturing, we conclude that structural shifts in the economy will probably require, on the average, more rather than less education of employees than in the past.

It is not clear that young people need a great deal of education and training for the jobs they will hold while they are young. According to analysis of the spring 1981 survey of the National Longitudinal Surveys (NLS) of Youth Labor Market Experience (Borus, 1983), about 28 percent of the jobs held by people ages 16-21 required only an elementary-school education. Just over half required less than a high-school diploma, about 14 percent required a diploma, and 7 percent required some college education.

According to the NLS, almost half the jobs held by people ages 16-21 required no more training than a short demonstration, 22 percent required less than 30 days of on-the-job training, and another 19 percent demanded no more than three months of training. This means that 87 percent of the jobs required less than 3 months of training.

It is not safe to conclude from these data, however, that young people do not need or would not benefit from more education and training. Given the aspirations of most people to advance in their careers and given the structural changes in the economy affecting the skills required in jobs, it may well be that young people need better education and training to prepare for their careers. The jobs they hold as teenagers or young adults are likely to require less education and training than the jobs they will hold later.

TABLE 2   Percentage Distribution of Employed People, by Employment Sector and Number of Years of Education

Sector	Years of Elementary and Secondary School		Years of College		Years of Graduate Work
	0-8	9-12	1-2	3-4	1-2
Manufacturing	28.8	57.7	3.0	6.0	4.0
Services	15.1	45.6	10.5	15.3	13.6

SOURCE: Stanback et al. (1981: Table 4.9). Reprinted by permission.

Technological Changes in the Workplace

Virtually no part of the U.S. economy has been untouched by technological advances. One indication of the pervasiveness of technological change is the September 1982 issue of *Scientific American*, which is devoted entirely to the mechanization of work. Among other topics, the articles discussed the mechanization of agriculture, mining, design and manufacturing, commerce, and office work. Vocational education programs are available in all of these areas. The importance of technological innovation for vocational education programs can scarcely be overestimated.

While all agree that the nature of jobs changes as a result of technological innovation, there seems to be little agreement among analysts regarding the likely nature of those changes over the next 20 years or so and their effects on the education and training required for the new or altered jobs. On one side are those who argue that the adoption of technological innovations will increase the skill levels required for jobs (Ayres and Miller, 1981). They argue that the workers so displaced will be the lower-skilled workers and that the newly created jobs will require more sophisticated technical training or managerial or other typically white-collar skills. (Whether the workers who are displaced can be retrained for the new jobs that would presumably be created is another question.) On the other side are those who believe that the widespread use of computerized systems will routinize jobs and increase the demand for low-skilled workers (see Levin and Rumberger, 1983; Vedder, 1982). Levin and Rumberger note that, while the fastest growth may be in computer-related occupations, the figures on percentage growth may be misleading because such jobs account for a very small proportion of the total work force. They cite figures from the U.S. Department of Labor projecting that 150,000 new jobs for computer programmers would be created in the 1980s; however, the estimate for janitors, nurse's aides, and orderlies is 1.3 million new jobs. They argue further that most of the jobs altered by computers will require only the most rudimentary of skills and certainly no high level of competence with computers. As computers become more sophisticated, those who use them can be less sophisticated.

The potentially disruptive effects of the automation of manufacturing on workers has been aptly described by the National Commission for Employment Policy (1982:7):

Workers may be threatened in the short term by loss of their jobs due to rapid automation of manufacturing plants and in the long term by the possible crippling of whole industries if manufacturers fail to automate rapidly enough or otherwise change their production techniques or wage costs to meet foreign competition. That the nation's unemployment rate exceeded 10 percent for the first time in 4 decades in September 1982, reflects not only the current recession, but also the disappearance of thousands of jobs in traditional "smokestack industries" such as iron, rubber, and steel, as well as in automobile manufacturing and other basic industries. Many workers in these industries who previously enjoyed both security and high salaries have consequently been left without work *and often without applicable skills* to compete in an emerging high-technology economy [emphasis added].

The potential effects of technological change on jobs are much more complex and pervasive than they may at first appear. The work of assembly-line employees, product designers, inventory clerks, managers, and executives can be revolutionized. Gunn (1982) notes that adopting new methods in one part of the manufacturing process has implications for other parts and for the cost and efficiency of the entire process. For example, using computers to facilitate the design of products is estimated to improve productivity in the drafting room by a factor of three or more. In addition, it results in higher-quality components that can be assembled faster and more easily and that ultimately result in a better product.

The increasing use of robots in industry raises concerns about the displacement of workers and the reshaping of training programs. Industrial robots are not the humanlike androids seen in science fiction movies. Instead, they are machine tools that can be programmed to move parts or tools through a specified series of motions. Some robots can be reprogrammed to perform different tasks without changing their hardware. Robots are best used in highly structured manufacturing situations in which there is virtually no variability or need for making decisions. The most common current applications include spot welding, spray painting, and loading and unloading metal cutting or forming machines, all of which have historically been taught in trade and industrial programs in vocational education. Robots are valued because of their predictability, reliability, and relative insensitivity to unpleasant environments. One of their major disadvantages is that, unlike humans, they are unable to react to unexpected situations or changes in their routines or environments, and they do not learn from past experience. Although robots are available that have rudimentary "senses" of sight and touch and that "learn" in a limited way, they are not yet commonly used in industry.

The Robotics Institute of Carnegie-Mellon University surveyed the members of the Robot Institute of America (robot users and producers) regarding their use of robots in various occupations, almost all in metalworking (Ayres and Miller, 1981). The results showed that robots are used most in nine occupations, which currently employ 3 million workers. A predicted half million of these workers could potentially be replaced by the type of robots currently used in industry. The most severely affected would be production workers engaged in welding, painting, and operating machine tools. One million more could possibly be replaced with the more sophisticated sensing robots. The researchers estimate that as many as 3 million workers in the areas of assembling, packaging, grinding, electroplating, and inspecting could potentially be replaced by sensing robots but that this displacement would take at least 20 years. They also note that six metalworking occupational categories for which vocational education offers training are likely to be seriously affected by robotization. These six categories accounted for approximately 3 percent of all vocational education enrollments in 1978 (almost a half million students).

While some believe that the widespread use of robots will lead to unemployment, others are not convinced and focus instead on the retraining of workers displaced by robots. As noted in a staff report on robotics and the economy prepared for the Joint Economic Committee of the U.S. Congress, "the challenge to policymakers due to increased use of robots is not unemployment but retraining" (Vedder, 1982:2). Vedder argues that robots will not increase unemployment but will instead improve productivity and thereby create more jobs. He reasons that the people who will be displaced by robots can be retrained to manage them or repair them or to do other production jobs that cannot be accomplished by robots.

Others see potentially far-reaching and long-term benefits of the increased automation of American industry (National Commission for Employment Policy, 1982). If manufacturers can decrease the price of goods by increasing the efficiency of production, the demand for such products could actually increase employment. (But the skill requirements of the new jobs, of course, would differ from those of the old.) If robots assume the most difficult and dangerous jobs, working conditions for people could be improved. In addition, automation could help to restore America's industrial base.

Regardless of which analysis one prefers, there are education and training implications for educators and students as well as the people currently employed in affected industries. Clearly, educators should maintain close contact with employers who use or are likely to begin using robots to determine the training implications for their programs.

Changes in the ways in which information is processed are also affecting a large portion of jobs in the U.S. economy. The National Commission for Employment Policy (1982) cited one estimate of the pervasiveness of telecommunication and computer technologies on occupations: approximately 55 percent of all U.S. workers in 1980 were employed in information-related occupations—generating, storing, transmitting, or manipulating data. The effects of changes in information processing on jobs and their skill requirements are complex and changing. For example, file and billing clerks and operators of older office machines are finding themselves with obsolete skills, while computer programmers and installers of cable television lines are in high demand. Yet not all computer-related jobs are increasing in number. As computerized equipment becomes more sophisticated, some of the earliest computer-related jobs, such as keypunching, are being phased out.

Some analysts view these technological changes with great optimism, both for specific geographic areas and for the health of the entire U.S. economy. A report on economic trends in New York City (Design for Academic Progress for the 80's Task Force #5, no date) expresses the view that jobs created by the "information revolution" can help revitalize the economy of that city. The jobs that have expanded in the last decade or so in New York City have been related to the creation, processing, and distribution of information—the media, telecommunications, printing, publishing, banking, insurance, the stock market, and others. The report notes that, although New York has lost many of its routine manufacturing jobs to overseas locations such as Hong Kong and Taiwan, the knowledge-intensive components of those industries—managing, design, marketing, and clerical work—have remained in New York. Thus, the nature of the jobs in the city has changed and has resulted in a change in the skills needed from employees. The need for unskilled workers has been reduced and that for technically skilled workers has increased, posing a challenge to the education system to train residents to fill the newly created jobs.

In order to learn about current practices in education and training relating to automation in manufacturing, the Office of Technology Assessment conducted a survey in 1982 of firms likely to use programmable automation in manufacturing (those making electric and electronics equipment, industrial machinery, and transportation equipment); producers of programmable automation equipment and systems; and educators and others involved in instruction, including labor unions. Results of the survey are reported in a technical memorandum (Office of Technology Assessment, 1983). About 40 percent of the manufacturing firms use programmable automation and about 22 percent sponsor or conduct training in the new technologies. Of those who do not offer training, only about 18 percent plan to do so in the future. This figure, the report notes, seems surprisingly low, given that virtually all the respondents—manufacturers and those involved in education or training—felt that industries should bear the cost of training employees to work with the new technologies. This finding could indicate that, while industries are reluctant to conduct their own programs, they are willing to pay for training conducted by others. Alternatively, it could mean that the changes in jobs caused by automation are not yet sufficient to warrant establishing formal training programs.

Youth Unemployment in the 1980s

According to the Bureau of Labor Statistics (BLS), in 1982 the annual average unemployment rate for the country as a whole was 9.7 percent, and the rate for people ages 16-19 was 23.2 percent. The unemployment rate for blacks in that age bracket reached a staggering 48.0 percent and that for people of Hispanic origin was 29.9 percent (see Table 3). These 1982 figures represent a seasonal adjustment of the monthly data gathered in the Current Population Survey of households across the United States.

Table 4 gives the 1982 BLS figures for people ages 16-21, showing a slightly different picture. The unemployment rate for the entire civilian labor force for that age group is 20.5 percent, while that for blacks and others is 38.5 percent. The figures are lower than those cited above because people ages 20 and 21 as a group are unemployed less often than those ages 16-19. Of those ages 16-21 who report that their major activity is going to school, almost 24 percent are unemployed. The corresponding figure for blacks and others is 47.3 percent. Of those unemployed while in school, most are looking for part-time work—about 85 percent of whites and about 74 percent of blacks and others. While it is undoubtedly true that many students who are looking for work are doing so primarily so they can have more spending money, there are also some who need the money to support themselves or their families for whom the lack of a part-time job is quite serious.

TABLE 3   Annual Unemployment Rates by Gender, Age, and Race or Ethnic Origin, 1981 and 1982 (Household Data)

	Total	White	Black	Hispanic
Total, age 16 and over				
1981	7.6	6.7	15.6	10.4
1982	9.7	8.6	18.9	13.8
Ages 16-19				
1981	19.6	17.3	41.4	24.0
1982	23.2	20.4	48.0	29.9
Males, ages 16-19				
1981	20.1	17.9	40.7	24.3
1982	24.4	21.7	48.9	31.2
Females, ages 16-19				
1981	19.0	16.6	42.2	23.5
1982	21.9	19.0	47.1	28.2

SOURCE: Bureau of Labor Statistics, 1983, *Employment and Earnings* 30(1) January: Table 51.

TABLE 4   Employment Status of the Noninstitutionalized Population Ages 16-21, Annual Averages for 1982 (Numbers in Thousands)

	Total	White	Black and Other
Total noninstitutionalized population	24,690	20,520	4,170
Total labor force	15,240	13,233	2,007
Percent of population	61.7	64.5	48.1
Civilian labor force	14,547	12,706	1,841
Employed	11,561	10,429	1,132
Agriculture	557	524	33
Nonagricultural industries	11,005	9,905	1,100
Unemployed	2,986	2,227	709
Looking for full-time work	2,018	1,499	519
Looking for part-time work	968	778	190
Percent of labor force	20.5	17.9	38.5
Not in labor force	9,450	7,287	2,163
Major activity going to school			
Civilian labor force	3,476	3,100	376
Employed	2,646	2,448	198
Agriculture	119	115	4
Nonagriculture industries	2,527	2,333	194
Unemployed	830	652	178
Looking for full-time work	142	96	46
Looking for part-time work	688	556	132
Percent of labor force	23.9	21.0	47.3
Not in labor force	6,397	4,973	1,432
Major activity other			
Civilian labor force	11,071	9,607	1,465
Employed	8,915	7,981	934
Agriculture	437	409	29
Nonagricultural industries	8,478	7,573	905
Unemployed	2,156	1,625	531
Looking for full-time work	1,876	1,403	473
Looking for part-time work	280	222	58
Percent of labor force	19.5	16.9	36.2
Not in labor force	3,053	2,313	740

SOURCE: Bureau of Labor Statistics, 1983, *Employment and Earnings* 30(1) January: Table 7.

The BLS unemployment figures cited above, which are the ones most often seen in the media, are calculated by dividing the number of unemployed individuals by the number in the labor force—that is, those either working or looking for work. Using instead ratios calculated by dividing the number of employed people by the total population for a given group gives a rather different picture, because of differences in the proportion of people in any group who are in the labor force. Table 5 gives employment/population ratios by age and race for 1981 and 1982. In all groups there are at least modest decreases in the employment ratios between 1981 and 1982. All people ages 16-19 are employed at about 60 percent the rate for the population as a whole, at least in part because the teenagers are in school. The teenagers may lack the skills for available jobs or they may not be able to work the hours required because of conflicts with school schedules. The employment/population ratio for black and other teenagers ages 16-19 is about half that for whites in the same age group. If we focused instead on unemployed people and calculated unemployment/population ratios, we would find that the difference between white teenagers and black and other teenagers is markedly smaller than that difference in the BLS unemployment rates cited above. These differences are attenuated by the differences in the proportions of the two groups that are in the labor force: proportionately fewer blacks and others ages 16-19 are either working or looking for work.

Analysis of a different data set, the spring 1981 survey of the National Longitudinal Surveys (NLS) of Youth Labor Market Experience, enriches our picture of youth unemployment. This section draws on a paper prepared for the committee by Michael E. Borus (1983). Selected tables from this paper are presented in Appendix A.

The unemployment rate for this group, composed of people ages 16-21 at the time of the interview, was 20 percent, a slightly higher rate than that found for the same time period in the Current Population Survey by the Bureau of Labor Statistics. The figure from the NLS implies that about 3.5 million young people ages 16-21 were unemployed in spring 1981. Although the unemployment rate for young men was generally higher than that for young women, some groups of young women have especially high

TABLE 5   Employment/Population Ratios by Age and Race for 1981 and 1982 (Household Data)

	1981	1982
Total	.70	.67
Total, ages 16-19	.44	.41
White, ages 16-19	.48	.45
Black and other, ages 16-19	.23	.21

SOURCE: Bureau of Labor Statistics, 1983, *Employment and Earnings* 30(1) January: Table 2 and Table 6.

unemployment rates: blacks; high-school dropouts; those with less than a high-school education; those who were married, divorced, or separated; those with children in the household; and those in the Northeast. Borus also found that the rate of unemployment declines as the young people grow older: 16-year-olds have a 31 percent unemployment rate, compared with a 13 percent rate for 21-year-olds.

Borus's analysis revealed a direct relationship between unemployment rates and lack of schooling, indicating that young people who drop out of high school have greater difficulty finding jobs than do their peers who graduate. High-school dropouts have extremely high unemployment rates—37 percent for female dropouts and 29 percent for male dropouts. They are often seen as lacking the skills, discipline, and motivation necessary to hold jobs. The unemployment rates for high-school students are only slightly lower—26 percent for females and 29 percent for males. Presumably students have difficulty getting jobs, in part because the hours they can work are constrained by their schooling and study.

The less education young people have, the more trouble they have in the labor market. The unemployment rate for those ages 16-21 with less than one year of high school was 40 percent in the NLS sample; the rate for those who had not finished high school was 28 percent; and it was 15 percent for high-school graduates. Those who had completed college (albeit a very small group of those ages 16-21) was only 3 percent. These findings are consistent with those of Meyer and Wise (1982a, 1982b) and Ellwood and Wise (1983).

Unemployment rates for minority young people in the spring 1981 NLS sample are higher than those for whites. The rate for blacks was 37 percent; for Hispanics, 24 percent; and for whites, 18 percent. Blacks constituted 23 percent of the unemployed but only 14 percent of the population of those ages 16-21.

As might be expected, youth unemployment rates are generally higher in localities with higher unemployment rates for the population as a whole and lower in areas with lower overall unemployment. Borus's analysis fails to support the commonly held view, however, that youth unemployment is highest in inner cities. Borus found that the youth unemployment rates in central cities of standard metropolitan statistical areas (SMSAs) are approximately the same as the rates in the areas of SMSAs outside the central cities. As we shall see below, however, the central cities have a higher percentage of hard-core unemployed young people.

Borus defined the hard-core unemployed as those who were out of school, who live either on their own or in a household in which the family income is below the poverty level, and who have been looking for work for 10 or more weeks. About 9 percent of the unemployed meet this definition.

There were about as many men as women, but there were few 16- or 17-year-olds. There were about equal numbers of people ages 18, 19, 20, and 21. The rates did not vary greatly by race or ethnic background. About 21 percent of those with no education past the eighth grade were classified as hard-core unemployed, compared with 5 percent of those with some high-school education (presumably many of whom were still in school), and 14 percent of those who had graduated from high school. Of those unemployed, 13 percent in the central city of an SMSA were hard-core unemployed, compared with 6 percent of those in an SMSA but not in the central city.

What factors tend to distinguish discouraged workers—those no longer looking for work presumably because they believe no jobs are available—from the young people who are looking for work? In Borus's analysis, more discouraged workers were dropouts and fewer were high-school graduates. Proportionately more lived in the South, in rural areas, or outside SMSAs. They tended to be concentrated in areas with high unemployment rates for the population as a whole.

The NLS sample includes questions of the young people regarding their reasons for looking for work, the types of jobs they sought, the lowest wage they would accept, and their perceptions of barriers to employment. About half the young people said they were looking for work because they needed money. An additional 20 percent had either lost or quit their previous job. Only about 7 percent said they needed to support themselves or help with family expenses.

Not quite half the young people who were unemployed were looking for full-time jobs. They tended to be older and not in school.

The NLS queried young people about their perceptions regarding the main reasons for their own unemployment or difficulties in getting a good job. About 45 percent of the respondents said they had been affected by age discrimination, the percentages understandably declining as the age of the respondents increased. High-school dropouts who were 16 or 17 years old perceived age discrimination more frequently than other groups. Sex discrimination was cited by 14 percent of the young women and 5 percent of the men. About 20 percent of the blacks and Hispanics felt that they had suffered racial or ethnic discrimination.

Lack of transportation was the most frequently mentioned structural barrier to employment, cited by 30 percent of the young people. Lack of experience was cited by 14 percent of the sample. Interestingly, lack of experience became a more commonly cited problem for the older respondents. Lack of education was said to be a problem by 6 percent of the sample overall and by 21 percent of the high-school dropouts.

In general, Borus's analysis of the NLS data on youth unemployment reveals that unemployment among Americans ages 16-21 is concentrated among certain groups. The groups with the highest unemployment rates include 16- and 17-year-olds, blacks, Hispanics, and high-school dropouts. The jobs typically held by young people require little education or specific training. One cannot conclude from this analysis, however, that education and training are unimportant factors in youth unemployment. Unemployment rates tended to drop with increasing educational attainment, suggesting that education and training are important in helping young people prepare for jobs.

Factors Contributing to Youth Unemployment

Finding jobs may be difficult for young people for a variety of reasons. They may lack basic skills (such as facility with spoken and written English, with reasoning, and with basic mathematical computations). They may lack the general or specific skills demanded in certain jobs. They may lack appropriate work habits and attitudes. And they may not have contacts with employers or know how to locate suitable jobs and apply for them. Some young people may be handicapped by deficits in one or another of these areas, and others may be deficient in several or all of them.

To read with understanding, to write clearly, to speak and listen effectively, and to perform basic mathematical computations are abilities generally considered essential to adequate performance in many if not most jobs today. These same abilities are necessary to satisfactory performance in most postsecondary education programs, which young people may choose in lieu of employment or as a means to better jobs. While most would agree that the ability to interact knowledgeably with computers is an important communication or computation skill, whether it is a basic skill is open to debate. Certainly, familiarity with computers is an asset in many educational and employment settings, but it is far from a universal requirement for either education or employment in the early 1980s.

Virtually all agree that these basic skills should be taught to students in elementary and secondary schools and that a high-school diploma should signify competence in these skills (see, for example, the report of the National Commission on Excellence in Education, 1983, and the report of the Twentieth Century Fund, 1983). For many entry-level jobs, employers require a high-school diploma or a demonstration of competence in basic skills. Some jobs inarguably require those skills; in other cases, a high-school diploma may be a proxy for other attributes that employers want, such as reliability, ability to get along with coworkers, or willingness to accept the authority of a supervisor (Corman, 1980). Regardless of the reasons for these requirements or their validity, this committee is concerned that many young people lack the basic skills so often required in entry-level jobs. We are not alone in our concern. A report of the Task Force on Education for Economic Growth (1983) concludes that the poor quality of American education—its inadequate job of preparing students for work—threatens this country's economy.

Schools face immense problems in trying to keep their education programs—general, vocational, or academic—current at the elementary, secondary, and postsecondary levels. In this era of rapid technological change and its similarly rapid diffusion into virtually all aspects of life, it has been argued that the skills that constitute basic competence or functional literacy change. Not only have new occupations opened up and others declined markedly, but also many jobs that have existed for decades have changed in nature. In an increasing number of jobs, employees must be able to interact with computers on at least a rudimentary level. While not everyone must be able to program a computer, knowing how to interact with them (or with those who program them) is important in an increasing number of occupations. For example, secretaries who use word processors work most effectively and efficiently if they understand at least a little about how the central processing unit of the system works and "reasons"; real proficiency with such systems involves more than the rote following of rules in a users' handbook. Parallel statements could be made about many other computer-driven systems, such as industrial robots, computerized devices for the diagnosis of automotive problems, and computers used in banking.

The Center for Public Resources (1982) conducted a national survey of corporate, school, and trade union personnel to measure their perceptions of the competencies in basic skills needed by employees. The areas of competence listed in the survey included reading, writing, speaking and listening, mathematics, science, and reasoning. In general, corporate personnel identified deficiencies among employees in most job categories listed in the survey, while school personnel believed that their graduates were adequately prepared for employment in terms of basic skills. Corporate and union personnel reported a serious problem regarding mathematics, science, and speaking and listening skills, which the educators did not perceive. Most business and union respondents noted that basic skill deficiencies limit the possibilities of job advancement for employees. Most companies represented in the survey had not estimated the business costs of these deficiencies in their employees but believed them to be high.

The fact that employers think that schools have the responsibility for teaching basic skills has been documented in a survey sponsored by the Conference Board (Lusterman, 1977). While employers may be reluctant to teach their employees basic skills—that is, to provide education that they believe ought to be provided by the public schools—some do so. (Lusterman reports that about 8 percent of the 610 companies with 500 or more employees surveyed provide education in basic skills.)

The American Society for Training and Development has estimated that employers spend about $40 billion a year on education and training programs for employees; the figure includes fees for instructors, administrative costs, equipment costs, and employee travel expenses. The Center for Public Resources (1982) recommended collaboration between educators and employers to improve the basic skills of students. Such collaboration would complement collaborative ventures focusing on vocational education.

Some employers are increasingly reluctant to hire people directly out of high school and with no work experience. These employers believe they have no assurance that young people are responsible and reliable until they have a sound employment record. They feel that, while some teenagers have acquired these qualities at home or in school, many have not, and a high-school diploma offers no reasonable assurance that its holder will possess basic attitudes essential to good work habits. Supervised work experience during the school years appears to offer students an escape from this Catch-22 situation.

Clearly, high-school dropouts or other people with inadequate grounding in basic skills are handicapped with especially serious problems in seeking education and training for employment. A few programs—the Job Corps and the Youth Incentive Entitlement Pilot Projects, for example—have been aimed specifically at these groups and are discussed in Chapter 2. The Job Corps is a federally funded program for disadvantaged young people who are not employed. As a group, participants tend to have relatively low levels of education and employment, to be dependent on public welfare relatively often, and to have relatively high rates of arrest or conviction. In addition to vocational training, a fundamental component of the Job Corps program is remediation in basic education. Most participants in the program leave their homes to live in residential centers in order to remove the negative influences of their current environments. In addition to education the participants are offered a comprehensive set of services, including health care, health education, and counseling. Participants are encouraged to work toward a general educational development (GED) certificate, which is recognized by state educational agencies as equivalent to a high-school diploma. Many analysts credit the success of the program to education and training in a supportive environment. While some may think such a comprehensive program expensive, analyses have shown that the benefits of the program far exceed the costs under a wide range of assumptions and estimates (Mallar et al., 1980).

In the past, work experience programs for people with a history of employment difficulties have not had a strong training component. Many of the programs funded under the Comprehensive Employment and Training Act (CETA) fit that description. Now, in part because of the success of the Job Corps, it is generally believed that training is an essential component of such programs. Most programs today, including those outlined in the Job Training Partnership Act—the successor to CETA—combine training and work experience in their attempts to increase the employability of their participants.

As effective as the Jobs Corps, the Youth Incentive Entitlement Pilot Projects, or similar programs may be, however, it is important to emphasize that they are means of providing a second chance for people who were not successful in the regular system of public education. Most would agree that spending money on a second-chance program is better than leaving people to be dependent on welfare or to engage in criminal activities. The existence of successful remediation programs, however, does not decrease the importance of the public schools as the principal institutions to provide education and training.

CONCLUSION

The fact that approximately 3 million Americans between the ages of 16 and 21 were out of work in 1982 is a matter of grave concern. The lack of appropriate habits, attitudes, and requisite skills—both basic and job-related—contributes to the problem of securing jobs for both young and displaced workers. Public schools across the country can help in solving the problem, but only if they offer strong grounding for all students in basic skills and up-to-date occupational skills. All students, whether they plan to work immediately after high-school graduation or not, should be prepared to reenroll in education or training programs as necessary throughout their lives in order to update their job skills. Structural changes in the economy, especially those changes brought about by technological innovation, make the task of the schools harder, but a close link between schools and private-sector employers can help educational programs stay current.

2 Education and Training for Employment

Vocational education is defined in the Education Amendments of 1976 (P.L. 94-482) as "organized educational programs which are directly related to the preparation of individuals for paid or unpaid employment, or for additional preparation for a career requiring other than a baccalaureate or advanced degree" (20 U.S.C. 2461, Section 195). That is what we mean in this report when we use the phrase *vocational education*.

In some sense, however, all education can be viewed as having a vocational component: the skills most essential to working in the majority of jobs are also the most fundamental skills that all students should learn—being able to read, write, speak, reason, and compute. As Ginzberg (1982:75) notes, "An increasingly white-collar economy has no place for functional illiterates." This is not to say that vocational education should be limited to teaching basic skills. Quite the contrary, vocational education courses or programs can help students acquire occupational skills—which virtually all will need, at least in the most general sense. Most people will work at some time during their lives, even if they do not plan to do so immediately after high school. They should at school age be introduced to the variety of employment options available in the American economy and receive guidance on how to find appropriate jobs, how to apply for jobs, how to behave in a work setting, and how to upgrade their skills if they need to.

In this chapter we describe vocational education as it exists in the early 1980s—its programs, students, schools, and the administrative arrangements supporting it. We then review evaluations of vocational education

22

programs at the secondary and postsecondary levels, paying particular attention to their effects on the employability of graduates. We also briefly consider evaluations of the Job Corps, a federal program for disadvantaged people that includes a large training component; the Youth Incentive Entitlement Pilot Projects, which combine education and employment to help disadvantaged young people; and 70001 Ltd., a largely private effort to train and place disadvantaged young people in private-sector jobs. We identify characteristics that are associated with program success and effectiveness. Finally, we discuss the question of access to vocational education in order to determine whether those people who might otherwise have difficulty getting good education and training, and subsequently getting good jobs, can enroll and participate in beneficial vocational education programs.

VOCATIONAL EDUCATION IN THE 1980s

Vocational education provides occupational training to millions of people in many different types of educational institutions across the United States. In 1980-1981 (the most recent period for which data are available), the National Center for Education Statistics estimated that 16.9 million[1] people were enrolled in vocational education programs supported in part by the Vocational Education Act of 1963 as amended (Table 6). About 10.5 million students were enrolled in high-school courses or programs and about 6.4 million were in postsecondary or adult education courses or programs. (As the terms are defined by the Vocational Education Data System, postsecondary programs lead to an associate degree and adult education programs may lead to a certificate, a credential, or simply completion.)

It is generally agreed that the figures cited above give an inflated estimate of vocational enrollments, since they count people enrolled in just one or two vocational education courses as well as those enrolled in programs comprising of a systematic set of courses and possibly work experience. Of the 16.9 million vocational students, about 5.8 million were enrolled in programs designed to train individuals for specific occupations. Occupationally specific programs are offered in grades 11 and 12 as well as in postsecondary and adult education schools.

---

[1] This figure does not include students enrolled in the many institutions that are privately controlled. Including those students raises the total to nearly 19 million. However, information on students in programs not supported by the Vocational Education Act is sparse and is not included in our discussion.

TABLE 6 Enrollments in Vocational Education Programs and
Occupationally Specific Vocational Education Programs, by Program
Area and Level, 1980-1981 (Numbers in Thousands)

Program Area	Total	Secondary	Postsecondary and Adult
All programs	16,861	10,466	6,396
Agriculture	883	664	179
Distribution	930	378	551
Health occupations	950	192	757
Nonoccupational home economics	3,189	2,550	640
Occupational home economics	574	377	197
Industrial arts	1,900	1,894	5
Office occupations	3,615	2,081	1,534
Technical	506	34	472
Trade and industrial	3,222	1,344	1,877
Other	1,134	952	182
All occupationally specific programs	5,793	2,858	2,935
Agriculture	376	304	73
Distribution	560	287	273
Health occupations	455	96	359
Occupational home economics	256	167	89
Office occupations	1,969	1,043	925
Technical	389	20	369
Trade and industrial	1,728	904	825
Other	60	37	23

NOTE: Occupationally specific enrollments include students above grade 10 enrolled in
programs designed to train individuals for specific occupations.

SOURCE: National Center for Education Statistics, Vocational Education Data System,
unpublished data.

Programs

The vocational education programs supported with federal funds cover
education in the following categories identified by the U.S. Department of
Education's National Occupational Information Coordinating Committee:
agriculture/agribusiness and natural resources, business and office occupations, health occupations, home economics (both occupational and nonoccupational), marketing and distribution, technical occupations, and trade
and industrial occupations. Typical areas of study in these programs are
listed opposite. Industrial arts, which is not included in the list, is not an

Typical Areas of Study Under Eight Vocational Education Program Areas

---

Agriculture/Agribusiness and Natural Resources Education
Agricultural production, supplies and services, mechanics, products; horticulture; conservation and regulation; fishing and fisheries; forestry production and processing.

Business and Office Education
Accounting, bookkeeping; banking; business data processing; office supervision and management; personnel and training; secretarial; typing.

Health Occupations Education
Dental services; diagnostic and treatment services; medical laboratory technologies; mental health/human services; allied health services; nursing-related services; ophthalmic services; rehabilitation services.

Home Economics Education
Interior design; consumer and homemaking home economics (nonoccupational); child care and guidance management, and services; clothing, apparel, textiles management and production; food production, management, and services; home furnishings and equipment management, and production; institutional, home management, and supporting services.

Marketing and Distributive Education
Institutional management; marketing management and research; real estate; small business management and ownership; entrepreneurship; marketing of apparel and accessories, business and personal services, financial services, floristry, farm and garden supplies, food, home and office products, hospitality and recreation, insurance, transportation and travel, vehicles and petroleum, advertising.

Technical Education
Communication technologies; computer and information sciences; architectural, civil, electrical and electronic, environmental control, industrial production, quality control and safety, mechanical, and mining and petroleum technologies; biological, nuclear, and physical science technologies; fire protection; air and water transportation; graphic arts technology.

Trade and Industrial Education
Drycleaning and laundering services; brickmasonry, stonemasonry; carpentry; plumbing, pipefitting, and steamfitting; electrical and electronics equipment repair; heating, airconditioning, and refrigeration mechanics; industrial equipment maintenance; drafting; graphic and printing communications; leatherworking and upholstering; precision food production; precision metal work; woodworking; vehicle and equipment operation.

SOURCE: National Occupational Information Coordinating Committee (1982).

occupationally specific program but includes courses surveying occupations as well as metalworking and woodworking shop.

On the basis of enrollments in occupationally specific programs, the two most popular programs are business and office programs and trade and industrial programs, in which a total of more than 60 percent of all vocational education students are enrolled (Table 6). This pair of programs dominates enrollments at all levels.

At the secondary level the largest programs overall are nonoccupational home economics and trade and industrial programs. Young women in high school enroll predominantly in health, nonoccupational and occupational home economics, and business and office programs. Young men in high school enroll predominantly in agriculture, industrial arts, technical, and trade and industrial programs. At the postsecondary and adult levels, the programs with the largest enrollments are business and office and trade and industrial programs.

Members of minority groups enroll mainly in nonoccupational and occupational home economics and business and office programs—areas traditionally dominated by women. They also enroll, in moderately high numbers relative to their proportion in the population, in trade and industrial programs, an area traditionally dominated by men.

Vocational education programs generally start at the high-school level. However, career education, introduced 10-15 years ago, begins in kindergarten (see Bell and Hoyt, 1974). Where such programs are offered, elementary-school children are exposed to information about different sorts of jobs and careers with the intention that they begin early to think about them. Presumably with the help of guidance counselors, they can start to see the relationship between their school studies and jobs they might later take. Students who are not academically inclined might become interested in schoolwork in this way, becoming convinced of its importance and relevance; they then may be motivated to learn the basic skills they will later need. Worthington (1981, 1982) notes that emphasis on prevocational guidance and career exploration is important at the elementary-school level to provide both vocational and nonvocational students with the information necessary to make realistic career and education choices.

Work Experience

Another aspect of vocational education involves work experience. Two types of work experience programs are supported in part by federal funds: work-study and cooperative education programs. Another type of work experience is participation in apprenticeship programs, which are generally jointly sponsored by industries and unions.

Work-study opportunities are provided by local education agencies to full-time vocational education students who need money in order to begin or to continue their vocational education study. Students in these programs work for the local education agency or for another public or nonprofit private organization, not for private-sector, profit-making employers. Students are paid with vocational education funds, not funds from the employers. The intent of the program seems to be much more to provide students the opportunity to work for pay than to increase their work experience or work skills.

The second of the federal programs providing work experience and the much larger of the two is cooperative vocational education, which is intended to provide supervised work experience that is related to a student's school program. In the 1979-1980 school year, over 520,000 high-school students were enrolled in cooperative education programs (U.S. Department of Education, 1981). Cooperative education is not a program in the sense that agriculture or marketing and distribution is, but rather an arrangement, plan, or a method of instruction that can be applied in any occupationally specific program. In cooperative education, written agreements are made between the school and the employer regarding planned and school-supervised employment of vocational education students. The students hold paying jobs at the employer's place of business and also participate in classroom instruction relating to their occupational experience. Compensation is scaled either to the minimum-wage laws or to a student-learner rate established by the U.S. Department of Labor. These students are typically in school part of the day and at work 3-4 hours a day outside school in any of a wide variety of occupations. In the 1976 Education Amendments, priority was given to funding cooperative education programs in geographical areas with large numbers of school dropouts or high rates of youth unemployment.

Cooperative education is designed to offer considerable benefits to participating students in addition to the wages that they earn on the job (U.S. Department of Education, 1981). The intended benefits include an opportunity to try working in an occupation before taking a full-time job, facilitating the transition from school to work, fulfilling personal needs and goals, acquiring appropriate work habits and job skills, and establishing an employment record. Employers benefit from cooperative arrangements because they gain access to a pool of potential employees who can be trained at relatively low cost and who can be observed at work before a job offer is made. Schools may save money they would otherwise have to spend on equipment with which to train students, and by careful scheduling they may be able to enroll more students than they could if all students were in school full time.

Apprenticeship training is one of the oldest, and many say one of the best, methods of providing training for many skilled occupations. Apprenticeship programs provide specialized training in a skilled trade, craft, or occupation and on-the-job training. They are generally run jointly by employers and unions. Apprentices are taught a variety of skills so that they can move with relative ease within a set of related occupations. Apprenticeship offers several advantages for the young people who are able to enroll— they earn money while in training, they learn by doing, and they have direct contact with employers and regular workers at the work site while they are learning.

The Smith-Hughes Act of 1917, which commenced the federal role in vocational education, also provided partial reimbursement from federal funds for teachers of related training in apprenticeship programs. The Bureau of Apprenticeship and Training in the U.S. Department of Labor registers apprenticeship programs that meet certain standards, which, for example, set the minimum age of apprentices at 16 years; prohibit discrimination in selection, employment, or training; require a schedule of work and training; and require related studies of a minimum length, an increasing schedule of wages, proper supervision and evaluation of apprentices, and recognition of successful completion (Glover, 1982).

Vocational education schools sometimes provide some of the basic training but do not become involved in the on-the-job training in apprenticeship programs. Currently the most common arrangement requires that people work and train as apprentices for a specified period of time, after which they become journeymen.

Since the 1960s, apprenticeship programs have been criticized for discriminating against women and members of minority groups. Federal regulations to promote equal opportunity in the programs have reportedly resulted in gains for blacks in the construction trades (Glover, 1982), but membership in the construction unions has changed more slowly and the representation of minority group members in apprenticeship programs varies considerably by trade. The situation regarding women is different because, with the exception of cosmetology, apprenticeship training is generally available only in jobs traditionally held by men. Glover reports that some progress has been made in the enrollment of women in apprenticeship programs across the trades but that data on their retention and completion are not yet sufficient to judge the success of the affirmative action efforts.

There is also criticism that apprenticeship programs are too long and that too few have the flexibility to give apprentices credit for previous work or education. Some unions are working to modify apprenticeship systems so that completion of these programs should be determined on the basis of competency rather than time; progress toward this goal is slowed by competing demands for the personnel and financial resources necessary to make the required changes.

The Bureau of Labor Statistics estimated that almost 324,000 people were enrolled in apprenticeship programs at the end of 1979. An Office of Technology Assessment report (1983) cited unpublished BLS figures showing a steady decline in enrollments to a level of 287,000 in 1982. The report attributes the decline to reductions in public and private funding rather than to declining interest in apprenticeship programs. They also note that economic conditions in the industries that cosponsor the programs may also have contributed to the decline.

Students

How do high-school vocational students compare with students enrolled in general or academic (college preparatory) high-school programs? According to the National Center for Education Statistics (1981), they are more like the students in general programs than those in academic programs. Their fathers tend to have lower educational attainment than the fathers of academic students. They tend to score lower on standardized achievement tests than do academic students. They also tend to work more outside school during their school years than do academic students. Their work is related to their studies more often than is the after-school work of academic students.

As an explanation of the comparatively low scholastic abilities and socioeconomic status of vocational education students in secondary schools, Evans (1981) notes that high-school vocational education attracts those students who are not interested in or who are rejected by college preparatory programs. If vocational education is serving the populations identified by Congress, its students would indeed be expected to have lower scores on standardized ability tests and lower socioeconomic status than those high-school students planning to go to college.

Meyer (1981a, 1981b) found that blacks and Hispanics, on the average, take more vocational education in high school than do whites. However, among individuals with comparable scores on standardized achievement tests and with comparable levels of parental income and education, blacks and Hispanics in high school take far less vocational education than whites. This finding is consistent with the finding that among people with comparable scores on standardized achievement tests, blacks are more likely than whites to go to college (Meyer, 1981c; Meyer and Wise, 1982a, 1982b).

Vocational programs at the postsecondary level tend to serve a more heterogeneous clientele than at the high-school level. In public and private noncollegiate postsecondary schools, about 20 percent of the students are over 30 years of age. Proportionately more female than male students are under 20 years of age, and slightly more are between ages 35 and 39. Nearly all vocational students (91.7 percent) who are enrolled in postsecondary noncollegiate schools have completed high school, and some (27.7 percent) have some postsecondary education or even an associate or baccalaureate degree (National Center for Education Statistics, 1981).

Schools

According to the National Center for Education Statistics, almost 28,000 public and private institutions across the country offer vocational education. These include public comprehensive and vocational high schools, public area vocational centers at the high-school level, private high schools, public and private noncollegiate postsecondary schools, correspondence schools, two- and four-year colleges and universities, and state correctional facilities. Nearly two-thirds of the schools are at the secondary level, most of them public high schools. Nearly a quarter of the institutions were private noncollegiate postsecondary schools—often called proprietary schools, even though many are nonprofit institutions (National Center for Education Statistics, 1981).

Comprehensive is a label attached to what most of us think of as regular high schools; this term was used in the Smith-Hughes Act of 1917. The National Center for Education Statistics (1981:3) defines a *comprehensive high school* as "a general high school offering programs in *both* vocational and general academic subjects, but in which the majority of the students are *not* enrolled in programs of vocational education." A *vocational high school* is defined as "a specialized secondary school that offers a *full-time* program of study in both academic and vocational subjects and in which all or a majority of the students are enrolled in vocational education programs." An *area vocational center* is a secondary-level "shared-time facility that provides instruction *only* in vocational education to students from throughout a school system or region. Students attending an area vocational center receive the academic portion of their education program in regular high schools or other institutions."

In site visits to seven large cities, Benson and Hoachlander (1981) found that specialized schools such as vocational high schools and area vocational centers are popular with students and offer programs of generally higher quality than comprehensive high schools. They note that this may be caused in part by the decay of and violence in inner-city comprehensive high schools, which these students would otherwise attend. They also note that the specialized schools attract highly qualified students, many of whom go on to college. Admission to some specialized schools is highly competitive, and some of them require admission tests.

In some cities there is rivalry between the shared-time vocational schools and the comprehensive high schools (Benson and Hoachlander, 1981). Administrators of comprehensive schools are sometimes reluctant to let students take their vocational courses in shared-time facilities because they fear the loss of revenue. They may lose support directly, if resources are allocated by the numbers of students in a school (capitation funding), or indirectly by reductions of staff no longer needed to teach vocational courses. Benson and Hoachlander also observed in inner cities what is true of vocational programs across the country: Some programs have kept pace with technological advances and benefited thereby, while others are ill-equipped, understaffed, and poorly matched to the labor market. They concluded that the local economy is a determining factor in the success of vocational programs in placing students in jobs, suggesting that placement rates are not always the best measure of success of vocational programs.

Where are the institutions that offer vocational education? About 60 percent of the secondary schools offering five or more vocational programs were located in areas with populations under 100,000 (U.S. Department of Health, Education, and Welfare, 1978); only about 27 percent of the population lives in such areas. The distribution of postsecondary institutions is more even with respect to population density. From this information it is not safe to conclude, however, that small towns and rural areas are oversupplied with vocational schools and centers. Evans (1981) states that residents of rural areas seldom have access to vocational education for a large variety of occupations. Their high schools most often offer programs only in agriculture, business, and nonoccupational home economics. Rosenfeld (1981) notes that rural schools also cannot afford to offer programs that require expensive equipment. With cautions about economies of scale and lower pay scales in rural areas, he notes that on the average rural school districts spend less per pupil than urban school districts. He concludes that vocational education, because of its demands for relatively high expenditures and for flexibility to adapt to the changing labor market, is extremely limited in rural settings.

Similarly, community colleges in sparsely populated areas do not offer as great a diversity of programs as do those in urban areas. Obviously, sparsely populated areas cannot take advantage of economies of scale in providing educational opportunities to their residents in the same way as large metropolitan areas. Rural areas need to have more schools to serve fewer people and cannot support a large diversity of programs. Area or regional vocational schools or centers are often found in sparsely populated areas, serving several towns or communities in a relatively large geographical area.

Teachers

In 1978 there were more than 354,000 vocational education teachers at the secondary, postsecondary, and adult levels (National Center for Education Statistics, 1981). This figure represents an increase of more than 50 percent since 1972, reflecting the growth of vocational education programs and enrollments in that period. In 1978 nearly half these teachers (47 percent) taught at the secondary level, almost 20 percent taught at the postsecondary level, and about 32 percent taught at the adult level.

At the postsecondary and adult levels a larger portion of the teachers teach only part time, compared with those in high schools. The National Center for Education Statistics (1981) estimates full-time-equivalent positions by assigning a value of one-third to part-time teachers. At the secondary level, using full-time equivalents reduces the estimate of teaching staff to 84 percent of the total number of full- and part-time teachers for the 1978-1979 school year. At the postsecondary level the percentage is about 70 percent, and at the adult level it is about 43 percent. On the basis of these figures, one can compute the percentages of the part-time teaching staff at each level: secondary, 24 percent; postsecondary, 45 percent; and adult, 85 percent. Many of the part-time teachers hold regular positions in private industry (U.S. Department of Education, 1981).

Part-time teachers usually have contracts to teach certain courses, and most often these contracts are renewed yearly. By contrast, full-time teachers at all levels derive job security by attaining tenure. Regardless of the benefits of the tenure system, the fact that most high-school vocational education teachers are full-time employees, many of whom have tenure, reduces the flexibility of the secondary schools. In order to adapt vocational education programs and staff to changing occupations, high schools must rely much more on retraining their currently employed teachers than on getting rid of teachers with obsolete or unneeded skills and hiring teachers with the needed skills.

Administration

The public schools that provide vocational education are governed and operated by states and localities, but they are affected by federal as well as state and local policies. The final report of a study of vocational education by the National Institute of Education (1981) gives a detailed description of administrative arrangements, funding patterns, and federal priorities. Several points from that report that are particularly relevant to our study are outlined in this section.

The federal role in vocational education is defined largely by the Vocational Education Act of 1963 as amended. The amendments of 1976 contain explicit expressions of federal priorities for vocational education programs. They emphasize overcoming sex-role stereotyping in education and employment and serving certain groups better—American Indians, disadvantaged students in areas with high youth unemployment and school dropout rates, and bilingual students. The legislation authorized funds for remodeling or renovating facilities as well as constructing residential schools in urban and rural areas that are unable to undertake such projects on their own. The planning of programs receives increased emphasis and the importance of state and local advisory councils is stressed. Work-study and cooperative education programs also receive increased emphasis in the 1976 legislation. Provision is made for collecting data on programs and students that would allow for better evaluations and judgments of accountability of the programs. Many items that had been treated separately in the 1963 act were consolidated in the 1976 amendments, but nonoccupational home economics maintained its separate status.

The Education Amendments of 1976 require that all states receiving federal vocational education funds establish a state advisory council. The text of the legislation states that the majority of the council's members shall not be educators or educational administrators, but the 20 areas of expertise or interest listed for required membership are mostly in education: They include business, labor, economic development, corrections, and public and private vocational education at various levels (11 of the 20 categories).

Interestingly, state licensing and professional certification boards are not required by law to be represented on the state or local advisory committees. Yet vocational education must accommodate licensing and certification requirements in its programs if its graduates are to pass those examinations and work in compliance with the law or with professional standards.

The state advisory councils are charged with advising the state education agency in the development of five-year plans for vocational education within the state, in evaluations of vocational education, and in identification of vocational education needs within the state. Each local education agency that receives federal vocational education funds is also required to establish a local advisory council, again with broad community representation. The local advisory council's mandate is to advise the local education agency regarding local employment needs and the extent to which vocational education is meeting the training needs of the community.

These state and local advisory committees for vocational education could be contrasted with the state job training coordinating councils and the private industry councils, established by the Job Training Partnership Act (JTPA:P.L. 97-300). Under the act, both types of councils have more direct responsibility than the advisory councils in vocational education. The JTPA councils are not merely advisory bodies. The private industry councils, for example, are responsible for the development of the job training plan for the local area; most of their members come from the private sector. Other members represent educational agencies, organized labor, rehabilitation agencies, community-based organizations, economic development agencies, and the public employment service (Section 102 (a)(1) and (2)).

The Job Training Partnership Act outlines provisions for coordinating its employment training programs with the existing vocational education system. The act requires that its training organizations go first to the education agencies for the provision of education in the basic skills and that local and state education agencies be represented on the private industry councils and the state coordinating councils. The CETA system, which was replaced by the JTPA system, was most often separate from and independent of the public schools but sometimes arranged for training to be done by public vocational education programs. JTPA allows the state coordinating councils under its authority to assume some of the activities of the state vocational education advisory councils, established by the Vocational Education Act and its amendments.

The Education Amendments of 1976 and the Comprehensive Employment and Training Act Amendments of 1978 established national and state occupational information coordinating committees, which were charged with the development and use of state occupational information systems. The JTPA provides for continued support of these occupational information committees. These systems were designed to help state and local administrators plan vocational education programs to meet the demands for trained labor. Several states also received special funding to develop career information delivery systems to provide students and young people not in school with information they might need in planning their careers.

Funding

The purpose of the 1976 amendments to the Vocational Education Act of 1963 is to provide federal funds to assist states (Section 101):

(1) to extend, improve, and, where necessary, maintain existing programs of vocational education;

(2) to develop new programs of vocational education;

(3) to develop and carry out such programs of vocational education within each State so as to overcome sex discrimination and sex stereotyping in vocational education programs (including programs of homemaking), and thereby furnish equal educational opportunities in vocational education to persons of both sexes; and

(4) to provide part-time employment for youths who need the earnings from such employment to continue their vocational training on a full-time basis.

The funds appropriated under the authority of these amendments for 1979 are outlined in Table 7. In effect, each of the sectional allocations is a block grant that can be used for a wide variety of purposes; however, specified portions of the sum of the Section 120 and 130 allocations to each state must be used to provide vocational education for people with handicapping conditions, disadvantaged people, people with limited English-speaking ability, and people who are no longer in high school. In addition, some of these portions can be expended only on the difference between the costs of educating people from these groups and the costs of educating others—for example, the costs of modifying equipment or instructional materials for people with handicapping conditions.

TABLE 7   Federal Appropriations for Vocational Education, Fiscal 1979

Purpose	Appropriation
Basic grants (Section 120)	$474,766,000
Program improvement (Section 130)	112,317,000
Programs of national significance (Section 171)	10,000,000
Special programs for the disadvantaged (Section 140)	20,000,000
Consumer and homemaking education (Section 150)	43,497,000
State advisory councils (Section 105)	6,073,000
Bilingual vocational education (Section 183)	2,800,000
State planning (Section 102(d))	5,000,000
Smith-Hughes permanent appropriation	7,161,455
Total	$681,614,455

SOURCE: U.S. Department of Education (1981:Table 1).

Clearly there are constraints on the use of the federal money that affect its use for program improvement and extension. The National Institute of Education (1981) argues that the two sets of purposes—program improvement and extension, on one hand, and service to target populations, on the other—are incompatible. The report states (p. xxxvi):

If the purpose is to enable poorer districts to maintain programs of the same quality as those offered in wealthier districts, the poorer districts should not be expected to spend an appreciable portion of their Federal funds year after year on program improvement projects. Similarly, if Federal dollars are to be used to provide programs and services for students with special needs, it is unlikely that they would be deployed to improve and extend services.

The National Institute of Education report (1981) observed that the 1976 amendments do not include provisions that effectively channel funds to the purposes stated in the amendments. Tracing the actual uses of funds is extremely difficult, in large measure because it is seldom possible to distinguish federal from state or local money once funds are applied to specific purposes. Nevertheless, the report concludes that localities use only a small portion of their funds to improve programs. Less than half the funds for program improvement and supportive services (guidance and counseling for students and in-service training of teachers, for example) is used for improvement, and states generally provide more money for supportive services than for program improvement.

Overall federal funds account for about 10 percent of the total expended for vocational education throughout the country; the remaining 90 percent is supplied by state and local sources. However, the ratio of federal to state and local funds varies considerably by the purposes or uses of the funds. As noted above, although procedures vary somewhat across states, funds are allocated to secondary schools or programs generally on the basis of school enrollment or attendance. Such funding formulas, called capitation funding, at the secondary level generally do not accommodate factors such as program costs, the costs of modifying programs to meet the demands of the labor market or changing occupations, the costs of providing remediation to educationally disadvantaged students, and the like. Vocational program funding at the postsecondary level is most often more flexible and can take into account factors that affect program costs.

EVALUATIONS OF VOCATIONAL EDUCATION

How effective has vocational education been? A number of studies, some of them quite ambitious, have addressed this question and are reviewed in this section. But before we look in any detail at those results, there is a larger question to consider: How effective is American secondary education? The decline in the scores on college entrance examinations since the mid-1960s has been well documented and publicized (College Entrance Examination Board, 1977). Only in the last two years has the decline slowed or perhaps begun to reverse itself (*Washington Post*, September 22, 1982, A3).

Data from the National Assessment of Educational Progress deepen the worries about the quality of the high-school education this country's young people receive. Gadway and Wilson (1976) reported that 8 percent of white high-school students and an astonishing 42 percent of black students could be considered functionally illiterate. Martin (1981) summarized the results for the 1970s: While some gains were made by 9-year-olds, the results for 17-year-olds showed declines in mathematical skills, reading comprehension, and knowledge about science and social studies over the decade of the 1970s. These data support complaints by employers and college teachers about the lack of basic skills of America's high-school graduates in recent years. It seems that while the nation's elementary schools are doing as well as or even slightly better than in the recent past, the high schools are not preparing young people adequately for further schooling or for work. It is little wonder, then, that vocational education at the high-school level has become involved in concerns over teaching basic skills. There continues to be some tension between teachers of vocational education and teachers of general education over who should be responsible for providing remediation in the basic skills for vocational education students. All agree, however, that all high-school graduates need to have mastered the basic skills.

Vocational Education Programs

Most detailed studies of the effects of secondary vocational education show wide variation in the effectiveness of programs. Meyer (1981d) found no net increase in lifetime economic benefits across all programs. He did find, however, that some programs seem to give participants some advantage the first eight years after high-school graduation. Participation in business or office courses tends to raise the income of women during the first eight years after graduation but does not seem to have similar positive effects on the income of men. Enrollment in trade and industrial programs tends to generate initial gains in income for men following high-school graduation. The positive effects of office programs for women and of trade and industrial programs for men decline after the first few years. Course work in nonoccupational home economics is associated with a significant decrease in income for women in the eight years following high-school graduation, but there is no evidence that this is a causal effect (Meyer, 1981d).

The National Institute of Education (1981) concludes that there is insufficient evidence to support a conclusive statement regarding the effectiveness of nonoccupational home economics education. A few studies cited in that report do indicate that students' knowledge increases after they have taken specific home economics courses; however, since the courses are explicitly nonoccupational, no measures relating program completion to economic or occupational results are cited.

Grasso and Shea (1979a, 1979b) present evidence that vocational education tends to decrease high-school dropout rates, thereby potentially giving participants the long-term economic benefits associated with a high-school diploma. Lewis and Mertens (1981) also report that most studies show that vocational education reduces high-school dropout rates. They also cite evidence that work experience programs may help motivate students to stay in school.

Summarizing findings from many evaluations of vocational education, Lewis and Mertens report mixed but generally positive findings regarding the effectiveness of secondary vocational education in reducing unemployment, generally positive findings regarding whether graduates found employment related to their training, but inconclusive and even contradictory findings regarding the earnings and occupational status of graduates.

A comprehensive study evaluating the effectiveness of secondary-school vocational education in placing graduates in jobs related to their training was conducted by McKinney et al. (1981). The research was based on literature reviews, analysis of existing data, case studies in 7 states, and a mail questionnaire received from over 5,000 people in 62 local education agencies in the 7 states. The report stressed the importance of vocational educators—administrators, counselors, and teachers—working to help place graduating students in jobs related to their training. Additional factors that seem to distinguish successful programs from others include participation of students in vocational education student organizations, students' mastery of basic educational skills, and the appropriateness of the curriculum to the employment opportunities in the area.

A recent report from the National Center for Research in Vocational Education (Gardner et al., 1982) examined employment experiences associated with different concentrations of participation in high-school vocational education programs. Unlike most earlier evaluations, the report considered whether students had enrolled in extensive vocational programs or just in a few vocational education courses. Gardner and his colleagues also examined intervening factors, such as the methods of job search used, unionization, type of industry and occupation, and job tenure, which could affect earnings and could differ between vocational education graduates and others. In general they found that differences in the earnings of vocational and other students were attenuated by several conflicting factors: Students who concentrate in vocational programs tend to hold their jobs for a relatively long time and tend to work in industries that pay well, but they tend not to work in unionized jobs or to enroll in postsecondary education institutions as often as others.

The investigators attributed differences in the effects of vocational education for men and women to the different labor markets into which they move. Women who concentrate in vocational education in high school tend to go on to postsecondary schools less often than men. Concentrating in vocational education tends to help women more than men in moving into higher-paying jobs than those held by others of the same sex without vocational training. Vocational graduates tend to work longer hours and for more weeks per year than others, a fact that helps account for their higher average annual earnings.

A survey of manufacturers' views of vocational education was conducted by the National Association of Manufacturers (Nuñez and Russell, 1981). The findings must be interpreted with extreme caution because less than 40 percent of the manufacturers polled responded to the survey, and the report gives no information on which to judge the nature and extent of response bias. Over half the respondents indicated that their companies had benefited from vocational education, and about 60 percent said that graduates of vocational programs needed less training than did other new employees in similar jobs. In general, vocational education is more highly regarded in companies that are currently involved in collaborative projects with vocational education. Among various types of collaborative efforts (examples of which are discussed more fully in Chapter 3), respondents most favored providing work experience for vocational students.

There are far fewer studies of postsecondary vocational education, but they show somewhat more impressive, positive results, especially for blacks and for some program areas. Both Mertens et al. (1980) and the National Institute of Education study (1980) found lower rates of unemployment for graduates of postsecondary programs in business occupations, trade and industry, and technical areas than for people in nonvocational postsecondary programs or those with no postsecondary education. These two studies also showed that graduates of postsecondary programs are more likely than graduates of secondary programs to find employment related to their training. In general, studies of the earnings of postsecondary vocational education graduates have been inconclusive. Grasso and Shea's planning paper for the National Institute of Education study (1979a) reported benefits for postsecondary vocational graduates, but Mertens et al. (1980) concluded there was insufficient evidence to draw conclusions.

A word of caution regarding the results of evaluations of vocational education is in order. Vocational education is provided in many different institutional settings under a rather loosely coordinated system of control. The quality of programs and intensity of instruction vary considerably, even within a given occupational field. Many evaluations of vocational education, in which earnings of graduates of vocational programs are compared with earnings of control groups, do not seek to distinguish between the returns for the stronger and weaker programs. One exception is a study conducted by the National Commission for Employment Policy (1981). In that study, economic returns to graduates of area vocational schools or centers, which are generally assumed to be in the stronger set, were found to be higher than returns to graduates of vocational education programs in comprehensive high schools. Distinctions among programs are also made in several studies cited here (Meyer, 1981d; Meyer and Wise, 1982a, 1982b). Failure to account for differences in program quality, which results in showing only modest economic gains for all programs taken together, is a reason to question whether the evaluation studies estimate accurately the returns to the better-trained graduates.

The findings of evaluation studies may also be rendered somewhat ambiguous by the fact that some unknown proportion of vocational students enroll in vocational courses or programs for nonoccupational reasons—to learn how to run a household or to do electrical work, for example. These people may enter the labor force looking for work intentionally unrelated to their vocational education. We do not judge whether the development of avocational skills is an appropriate use of public funds, but the fact that vocational education serves this dual function renders evaluation of economic returns difficult.

Most of the evaluation studies focus on benefits accruing to graduates of vocational programs to assess the worth of vocational education. However, as Grubb (1979) notes, employers are often the primary beneficiary, since they can shift some of the costs of training employees (even in firm-specific skills) onto government. Thus, ignoring benefits to employers underestimates the value of vocational programs.

Other Training Programs

Assessment of the nature and effectiveness of several other employment training programs is relevant to the committee's work because of the emphasis they give to training their participants. The programs we cite in this section are the Job Corps, the Youth Incentive Entitlement Pilot Projects, and 70001 Ltd. Other federal employment programs, such as the Manpower Development and Training Act and other portions of CETA, have paid relatively less attention to training and instead have emphasized giving participants work experience, which has been shown to be less effective than classroom or on-the-job training in increasing postprogram earnings (Bassi, 1982). The Job Training Partnership Act, which continues the support of the Job Corps, emphasizes training in its other programs as well.

The Job Corps is a federally funded program aimed at reducing unemployment among disadvantaged, unemployed, out-of-school young people ages 16-21. The Job Corps was originally established under the Economic Opportunity Act of 1964; later it was supported under Title IV of the Comprehensive Employment and Training Act of 1973. It operates about 100 residential training centers in which participants receive remedial education in the basic skills, vocational training, support services such as health care, and general preparation for work. A number of different organizations become involved in various aspects of the Job Corps program. International unions participate in recruiting, placing, and training participants. Employment services work in recruiting and placing participants. Local schools train participants under contract to the Job Corps centers. And volunteer or community-based organizations work to recruit and place participants in jobs and also to provide support services to them.

More quantitative data are available on the Job Corps than on most other federal training programs for disadvantaged people (Bendick, 1982).

Probably the most robust evaluations of the Job Corps have been conducted by Mallar and his associates (1978, 1980). The first evaluation (Mallar et al., 1978), which followed participants for seven months, showed that, on the average, Job Corps participants earned more per week than those in comparison groups and more of them obtained employment, attended college, or joined the military services. They also showed other benefits, such as better health, and reported reductions in criminal behavior and drug or alcohol abuse.

The second evaluation (Mallar et al., 1980), which followed participants for two years, showed an increase in the amount of employment, earnings, military enlistment, and the probability of getting a high-school diploma and a reduction in reliance on public assistance, such as unemployment insurance. These results seem even more impressive when one remembers that the Job Corps serves severely disadvantaged people—those most in need of help and those least likely to make similar attainments without such assistance. The notable success of the program is attributed largely to its emphasis on training and its provision of a supportive environment for participants.

70001 Ltd. is a nationwide private enterprise (which has received some money from CETA) that has grown from a privately funded project in Delaware in 1969. 70001 Ltd. serves high-school dropouts in 45 communities across the country. The participants, who have been screened on the basis of abilities and attitudes, agree to work toward specific individual goals. They are given a 2- to 5-week period of training in work habits and attitudes and job-seeking skills. Participants are encouraged to work toward a general educational development certificate. They participate in a national youth organization associated with 70001 Ltd., modeled after the Distributive Education Clubs of America (an organization for vocational education students), which provides peer-group and motivational support. The training for 70001 Ltd. programs is usually conducted by community-based organizations with assistance from the national 70001 Ltd. office.

A coordinator, determining that individual participants are ready for employment, arranges job interviews for appropriate occupations with private-sector employers. Coordinators try to ensure a good match between jobs and participants. The youth organization associated with 70001 Ltd. provides recognition for educational and occupational achievements, teaches organizational and leadership skills, and helps participants develop a sense of career and community awareness and responsibility.

Evaluations show generally positive results, including gains in earnings for 70001 Ltd. participants. An evaluation by Public/Private Ventures found that gains in earnings actually increased over time rather than declining, as is usually the case with such programs (Sullivan, 1983). About three-quarters of the enrollees complete the program, and about three-quarters of those who complete the program are placed in unsubsidized jobs in the private sector.

Another federally funded program is the Youth Incentive Entitlement Pilot Projects (YIEPP) demonstration, which was authorized by the Youth Employment and Demonstration Projects Act of 1977. This program combined education and work in order to help reduce youth unemployment, to increase labor force participation, and to reduce school dropout rates of teenagers. The target population was people ages 16-19 from low-income or welfare households who had not graduated from high school. The program offered each participant a guaranteed job at the federal minimum wage, part-time during the school year and full-time during the summer, provided the participant remained in or returned to school or worked toward a general education development certificate. Continuing participation in the program was contingent on maintaining both school and work performance standards. The program subsidized the jobs of participants, usually at a rate of 100 percent. At two sites, subsidies of 75 and 50 percent were tried to test the effects of varying subsidy levels on employers' willingness to participate. Participation of private-sector employers was found to be highly dependent on the level of subsidy offered. Employers were about four times more likely to participate with a 100 percent subsidy than with a 50 percent subsidy.

The YIEPP demonstration program began in spring 1978 and ended full-scale operations in August 1980. Over 76,000 young people participated in the program at 17 sites across the nation operated by competitively selected CETA prime sponsors. The program was evaluated by the Manpower Demonstration Research Corporation, which has issued a series of reports on the program. Two are of particular relevance to the current study (Diaz et al., 1982; Farkas et al., 1982). Selected findings of those evaluation reports are presented here. In general, the prime sponsors were able to secure jobs for all participants, but they did have some difficulty at a rural site in Mississippi. Overall the quality of the work experiences of the participants was judged adequate or better, meaning that the young people were kept busy, that they were held to their performance standards, that they received adequate supervision, that their work was varied, and that there was a low ratio of participants to supervisors. The quality of the work experience did not vary substantially among the private, public, and private nonprofit sectors.

Establishing and enforcing school performance standards for participants proved difficult and time consuming. However, anecdotal evidence suggests that enforcement of the standards gave the program needed credibility among school administrators. It also was used in several instances to effect the provision of educational remediation when students' performance declined. In general, cooperation between the schools and prime sponsors was good. Schools complied with monitoring requirements; they effectively recruited students for participation; and, as best they could, they provided flexible scheduling of classes to accommodate students' work schedules.

Application and participation rates in YIEPP were high, indicating the eagerness of disadvantaged young people to obtain minimum-wage jobs, even though that also meant adhering to performance standards and either going to school or pursuing an equivalency certificate. Of those who had heard about the program, about 80 percent had applied, and about 56 percent of those eligible at the beginning of the program had participated by its termination. Participation rates at the end of the program were 22 percent for whites, 38 percent for Hispanics, and 63 percent for blacks. Diaz et al. (1982) hypothesized that the greater participation rates for black and Hispanic young people may be attributable to the limited employment opportunities for them in the unsubsidized labor market. Analyses of youth employment data by Borus (1983) suggest such a limitation for black young people, particularly in jobs paying the federal minimum wage.

A Congressional Budget Office study (1982), citing Stromsdorfer (1979) and Taggart (1981), draws five major conclusions regarding a variety of employment and training programs for disadvantaged young people. First, considerable gains in employability can be made by young people who participate in programs offering remedial education, training, and well-structured work experience. The gains appear to be statistically related only to the amount of time spent in education and training, but work experience seems to act as a motivator for people to continue in the programs. Second, success in the workplace seems to be closely related to competence in the basic skills of reading, writing, speaking, and computing. Based on their analysis of data from the National Longitudinal Surveys of 1972 High School Seniors, Meyer and Wise (1982a) draw similar conclusions regarding the importance of basic skills. Third, work experience alone, even when well supervised and highly supportive, does not appear to improve the employability of disadvantaged young people. To be effective, work experience must be combined with other services, such as skill training and placement services. Fourth, to be effective, programs must be well managed, and participants who do not conform to minimal standards of behavior should not be allowed to continue in the programs. Fifth, placement services and training in how to look for a job seem to increase the short-term employability of program participants. The work of Gardner et al. (1982) confirms this fifth conclusion for vocational education high-school graduates.

We conclude, therefore, that there is ample evidence that well-constructed training programs—ones that ensure a firm grounding in the basic skills, that provide supervised work experience, and that provide sufficient motivation for participants to complete the programs (usually through work experience)—offer promise for improving the employability of disadvantaged young people. We can infer that dislocated workers who participate in programs offering the same elements, though perhaps with different emphases, would profit similarly.

Access to Vocational Education Programs

A major concern that shaped the 1976 reauthorization of the Vocational Education Act of 1963 was ensuring access to vocational education programs for those individuals who were likely to have trouble getting a job without that training or support, especially those people living in places with high unemployment rates or other indications of economic need. Congress wanted to ensure, first, that there were good vocational education programs in places where people were in particular need of training and, second, that those people who needed the training could enroll in programs likely to improve their employment prospects. Thus we examine two aspects of access to programs: first, the distribution of funds to localities in greatest apparent need, and second, enrollment in high-quality programs.

In their study of the effectiveness of vocational education programs for the National Institute of Education, Benson and Hoachlander (1981) found in the 12 states studied that the distribution of federal funds to local education agencies was not effective in meeting those congressional concerns. Even in the seven states in which federal funds were directed properly to local education agencies with below-average relative financial ability (i.e., property value per unit of average daily school attendance), above-average unemployment rates, and above-average concentrations of low-income families, the pattern was not consistent across areas. The six states studied at the postsecondary level did not consistently allocate funds according to the criteria set by the federal government.

Benson and Hoachlander (1981) studied enrollment patterns as well as the distribution of funds. They reported that women are concentrated in vocational programs that rank low in employment opportunities and average expected wages. The same pattern holds, though much less strongly, for members of minority groups. They concluded that, in large cities, access to high-quality vocational education programs for various target groups—minorities, women, people with handicapping conditions, economically disadvantaged people, and students with limited English proficiency—is often limited.

They cited four reasons for this limited access. First, some of the programs are geographically isolated; programs may be offered in facilities far from the neighborhoods in which members of minority groups or disadvantaged students live. Second, limitations may be placed on program enrollments. The combination of insufficient funds to expand programs and intense competition for the most popular programs may tend to exclude students who do not possess the basic skills needed and virtually to eliminate the incentives for the programs to offer remedial education. Sometimes, too, program enrollment is restricted to match labor market demand. Third, program admission requirements may exclude proportionately more disadvantaged students, even though this exclusion may be unintentional. Admission requirements may include scores on standardized ability or intelligence tests, grade point average, school attendance record, and personal characteristics. Some programs may also require certain course work. Fourth, perceived restrictions in job entry may deter some students from applying to some programs. For example, female, black, or Hispanic students may avoid programs leading to careers in which they see that employers seldom hire others like themselves. This avoidance, of course, perpetuates the problem of underrepresentation of those groups in those occupations.

As we observed earlier, it is not just large cities that face difficulties in offering enough good programs to students. The provision of a variety of high-quality programs in rural areas is also very difficult because sparsely populated areas cannot take advantage of economies of scale in establishing and operating programs (Rosenfeld, 1981).

CONCLUSION

We conclude this chapter as others who have studied education have done—with a mixture of optimism and grave concern. We believe we know what is important for vocational education students: mastery of the basic educational skills, exposure to a variety of occupations, mastery of the basic occupational skills, adoption of appropriate work habits, and participation in well-supervised work experience that is closely related to the school studies. Like others before us, we believe we know success when we see it, but we have no formula for making all programs successful.

As this chapter notes, entry into the most effective vocational programs is highly competitive. Those students who have not mastered the basic educational skills or who have not developed disciplined work habits cannot compete effectively for places in the programs. Because of the high demand for places, high-quality vocational programs have no incentives to offer remedial education to students who need it. Those students may have to rely on generally effective but expensive programs like the Job Corps or 70001 Ltd. for their second chance.

From our reviews of vocational education programs and other employment training programs and from our collective experience with various aspects of such programs, we conclude that fundamental changes are needed to improve some vocational education programs to a significant degree. Those programs generally regarded as being most in need of improvement are often in public comprehensive high schools, and it is there that we concentrate our attention. We believe that those programs could be improved dramatically by strengthening the teaching staff and by increasing the flexibility of funding arrangements. We believe these changes, put forward in Chapter 4, are both desirable and possible, but we fully acknowledge that some of them will require enormous changes in institutions not noted for their willingness to change. Adoption of our recommendations will require considerable courage but should result in substantial improvement in educational and ultimately in employment opportunities for America's young people.

Evaluations of vocational education and other training programs fairly consistently show that supervised work experience in conjunction with education is important to success. This is the oldest and perhaps the best reason for collaboration between vocational education and business and industry, which is the subject of the next chapter.

3 Vocational Education and the Private Sector

In Chapter 2 we saw that close ties between schools and the workplace can benefit students. The vocational education programs that have higher economic and occupational benefits generally also have close and effective relationships with employers. Students who participate in supervised work programs while they are in school tend to fare better once they graduate and work on their own. Further support for this conclusion comes from experience with employment training programs outside the public education system: Virtually all of the effective special training and service programs designed for disadvantaged people operate in conjunction with employers—and some with unions and community-based organizations as well. Who initiates collaborative efforts? How do they work? What institutional or administrative arrangements do they require? What do they accomplish?

In this chapter we present information on collaborative efforts involving vocational educators and students and private-sector employers. We discuss a number of specific collaborative activities that have been viewed as successful and the institutional and administrative arrangements of the vocational education system that affect collaboration. We also discuss the role of vocational education in economic development efforts, principally the tailoring of education and training programs to meet the needs of employers moving into an area.

The collaborative efforts of principal concern to the committee are those linking high-school vocational education and the private sector that seek to improve the employability of students. All involve cooperation and communication between education and business, and many involve organized

47

labor, community-based organizations, chambers of commerce, and local government. Some of the material in our discussion has been drawn from a paper written for the committee by Sean Sullivan (1983), "Private Initiatives to Improve Youth Employment," which reviews several collaborative efforts.

EXAMPLES OF COLLABORATIVE PROJECTS

Up to this point this report has focused primarily on a traditional model of providing education and training for employment: students learning the basic education and occupational skills in public schools offering vocational education programs and gaining work experience at an employer's place of business. In this section we discuss the variety of forms collaborative ventures can take—the many ways employers and educators can work together to improve the education and employment experiences and prospects of students. We also describe a number of specific collaborative efforts that have been viewed as successful by those involved in the projects. We caution that judgments of success are not based on rigorous evaluations of program procedures or outcome measures but rather on the opinions of those who have worked with the projects or who have participated in them.

Different institutional arrangements for providing occupational education and training and different mechanisms for collaboration are appropriate for different situations. The variations involve who actually does the teaching, who pays the teachers' salaries, who pays for facilities and equipment, and where the facilities and equipment are located. In the case of new and expanding industries, it may be appropriate for employers to take the major responsibility for training students, since schools may not be prepared, in terms of equipment or teachers, to train entry-level employees for those industries. In such cases, employers can obtain the skilled workers they require by providing access to their facilities and equipment for instructional purposes. Employers can also provide their own personnel as instructors. These arrangements can be initiated by one firm or a combination of firms needing workers with similar skills.

If the industrial equipment is movable or exists in sufficient supply, employers may instead place the necessary equipment in the school. Under this arrangement, the intructors may be employees of the firm or they may be vocational education teachers from the school system.

Collaborative efforts offer several advantages to employers. They may participate in such projects in order to increase the pool of qualified workers from which they can draw. Such arrangements allow employers to screen the students before hiring them for jobs. They may also reduce job turnover, since the students learn what is expected of them on the job while in training, thus effectively reducing the employers' recruitment, hiring, and training costs.

Community-based organizations can often contribute significantly to collaborative ventures, particularly those aimed at young people who are economically disadvantaged or members of minority groups—the constituents of the organizations. Community-based organizations are especially valuable in recruiting eligible young people, developing jobs—perhaps with minority-owned or minority-operated businesses—and supervising work experience (SER/Jobs for Progress, no date).

Schilit and Lacey (1982) described 55 diverse programs involving collaboration between educators and private-sector employers. Although the evaluation data were not presented and the evaluations were generally not rigorous, all 55 programs were said by school administrators, teachers, students, and employers to have been successful at their particular goals. Most started with a small pilot effort, often initiated by a single firm or school, and grew to accommodate more students, schools, or employers. Some businesses became involved in additional projects after their initial experience with the schools. Most collaborative efforts relied on local initiatives; federal funding served as the impetus for very few. Most of the programs cited by Schilit and Lacey were not new. About one-fourth of the 55 projects had existed for 10-20 years; only 5 had started less than 2 years before the study.

In some situations, local chambers of commerce, business associations, or other organizations are needed to coordinate the efforts of several firms. For example, the Training Opportunities Program places junior and senior vocational students in part-time jobs throughout New York City. Business and labor advisers identify groups of jobs in small firms that are expected to contribute to the economic development of the area. The board of education supplies the funds for the salaries of the student workers (New York City Public Schools, no date; Schilit and Lacey, 1982).

In other places, students run their own businesses with assistance from established local firms. In Montgomery County, Maryland, for example, with the financial and technical support of local business executives and private foundations, vocational schools establish businesses that are run entirely by students. Students have constructed and sold houses, and they have operated a small automobile dealership. The profits they make are used to support the programs.

Collaborative efforts need not be limited to senior high schools, though that is the focus of this report. In Los Angeles, Atlantic Richfield (ARCO) "adopted" elementary schools and allowed several hundred employees to volunteer during working hours to tutor, conduct short courses, and supervise ARCO-funded field trips to businesses and cultural sites. Fonte and Magnesen (1983) reported on a cooperative program in which Triton College in Illinois and community colleges in other states served as training sites for the General Motors Automotive Service Education Program. Apprentice mechanics enroll in the two-year program to learn mathematics, electronics, communications skills, and a variety of automotive topics.

Not all collaborative programs at the secondary level are aimed at vocational students or have as their goal the teaching of vocational skills. For example, Kaiser Aluminum and Chemical Corporation established reading and math centers in the schools in Oakland, California, to help students master these basic skills (Levine and Doyle, 1982). The centers featured individualized instruction and tutoring from peers. Students who made the most progress in the learning centers were offered part-time jobs as a reward for their achievements.

In the following pages we describe nine examples of collaborative ventures that are generally viewed as successful. Material for these descriptions was drawn largely from Schilit and Lacey (1982), Sullivan (1983), and Robison (1978). The first three examples—Success on the Move, Opportunities Industrialization Centers, and the Career Intern Program— were developed by private parties but involve funding from either the U.S. Department of Labor or the U.S. Department of Education. The other examples do not involve federal funding; they are strictly cooperative ventures between business and education at the local level.

Success on the Move

In 1979 Kaiser Aluminum and Chemical Corporation worked with the high schools in Oakland, California, to create a program called Summer on the Move, which was designed to improve the basic academic skills of disadvantaged high-school students while giving them summer work experience in local businesses. In 1980 the program was expanded to a year-round operation, Success on the Move, through the efforts of Youthwork, Inc., a nonprofit organization, and a grant from the Edna McConnell Clark Foundation to test a private-sector/education partnership approach nationally. The program's curriculum emphasizes improvement of basic communication, computational, and problem-solving skills in ways that students can relate to work—skills that employers had identified as important in employment.

Participants in Success on the Move are given part-time and summer jobs with local employers. Work experience exposes them to the demands and discipline of a job, allows them to apply the skills they have been learning, and acquaints them with the kinds and requirements of entry-level jobs available. In the six-week summer program, students get classroom instruction in the morning and work in the afternoon. The school-year program involves an extra hour of daily classroom study plus an average of 10 hours paid work each week for 15 weeks. Students are selected through interviews and recommendations.

The difficulties encountered in developing this kind of cooperative venture include generating enough jobs; establishing and maintaining contact between employers and educators; and involving employers in planning, curriculum development, instruction, and evaluation.

Opportunities Industrialization Centers

Opportunities Industrialization Centers (OIC) is a network of over 100 organizations that provide employment training and other services to members of minority groups and to economically disadvantaged people across the nation (Robison, 1978). Each local center is an independent affiliate of Opportunities Industrialization Centers of America (OIC/A), located in Philadelphia, which provides technical and administrative assistance to the local centers. OIC was founded by the Reverend Leon H. Sullivan, who chairs the national board of directors of OIC/A. One distinguishing characteristic of OIC is its commitment to provide training only where guaranteed employment opportunities exist. A second is to serve the needs of the "whole person" by offering assistance in recruitment, counseling (including not only job-seeking skills and work habits but also basic skills education), prevocational training, vocational training, job development, and follow-up of individuals once they have jobs.

To ensure communication and commitment from businesses at the national and local levels, the National Industrial Advisory Council, composed of leading business people from diverse industries, was formed. The council helps inform businesses about OIC and helps keep OIC programs current. There are at the local level advisory councils corresponding to the national council. Firms belonging to the local councils help OICs by donating equipment and funds, lending supervisors and instructors, organizing fund-raising activies, and providing on-the-job training and jobs. OICs also give employers classes in awareness training so that supervisors can learn some aspects of the culture of the minority groups represented by the program participants with whom they will be working. Because OICs train for jobs that are known to exist, they develop and maintain close relations with employers and develop specialized training programs to meet their needs.

The Office of Vocational and Adult Education in the U.S. Department of Education is currently promoting the work begun by Sullivan and carried forward by the OICs. The office is currently running a national Task Force on Entrepreneurship Education and Training. One of its emphases is on management training for members of minority groups who own or operate small businesses.

The Career Intern Program

The Career Intern Program (CIP) was developed by Opportunities Industrialization Centers in cooperation with school boards in five cities, with funding by the National Institute of Education, as an alternative high-school program to keep potential dropouts in school. The first program was located in Philadelphia, and other sites were added after several years of experience at the first. Courses are coordinated with the regular public school system and stress basic academic skills and attitude improvement. Classes are held at sites away from the schools because the organizers believe (on the basis of evidence from the Job Corps) that the young people learn better outside traditional classrooms. The subjects taught are occupationally related, and classroom study is supplemented by visits to work sites. Interns are given intensive counseling as well as instruction to prepare them to behave appropriately in the workplace. As they accrue more credits, their course work contains more specialized career-oriented subject matter. They also spend more time at work sites observing and, where regulations allow, performing some tasks. As graduation approaches they are assisted in looking for jobs or enrolling in postsecondary institutions.

Sullivan (1983) notes that an evaluation of the program in Philadelphia found that participants were significantly more likely to stay in school than were members of a control group, and studies of the other sites concluded that the approach could be replicated. OIC has a design for implementing the Career Intern Program nationally, but funding from the National Institute of Education has been depleted and no new sources have been found.

The South Central Connecticut Regional Council
on Education for Employment

The South Central Connecticut Regional Council on Education for Employment begins the process of career education in elementary school. It grew from an earlier program, started by the Olin Corporation, to allow New Haven high-school vocational education students to learn work skills directly on the job. The Connecticut Foundation for School/Community Relations brought together firms, schools, and public agencies, with financial support from Olin and from the state department of education. A novel example of its efforts is the school-bank program, which involves nine banks working directly with nine inner-city classes of primary-school students and their teachers. The curriculum, developed jointly by teachers and bank staff, allows each class to spend several hours each week in the bank, using knowledge of arithmetic while learning about bank operations and using calculators and computer terminals. A three-year evaluation of this program found that participants had significantly higher math achievement levels than control-group members.

The St. Louis Work-Study Program

About 2,500 students have taken part in the St. Louis Work-Study Program since its inception in 1967. High-school students spend mornings on academic studies and afternoons on paid jobs. Both sessions take place at business locations. Students can explore careers, learn business skills and behavior, and gain experience on the modern equipment available in large firms. Conducting classes at the work site is thought to promote communication among teachers, work supervisors, and students; it also allows feedback on the relevance of the academic program to the job.

A grant from the Danforth Foundation helped establish the first partnership, between the schools and the Ralston-Purina Company, which still has the largest program: As many as 40 high-school seniors from inner-city schools participate each year. The St. Louis board of education assigns two teachers to the Ralston-Purina program, one to teach academic and the other business courses. Corporate personnel have the main responsibility for training and supervising students on the job, but the teachers remain on the site to help coordinate work experience with classroom instruction and to monitor students' job performance. Students are screened by the schools and matched with particular jobs and are paid the minimum wage for a 20-hour work week. They earn academic credit for the training as well as for the course work. Company supervisors—who are volunteers—rate the students after each of four 10-week periods on attendance, punctuality, work habits, skills and knowledge, attitudes, and personal characteristics. These ratings help the teachers to refine the curriculum and to work with students on individual needs. An average of 75-80 percent of the students have been placed annually, and another 15-20 percent have continued their education; the annual attrition rate is less than 5 percent.

The Continental-Illinois Bank

Continental-Illinois Bank in Chicago has employed more than 1,000 students in part-time jobs since the beginning of its work-study program in 1972. The bank has found work-study participants better motivated and better adjusted to the work world when they become full-time employees. The bank and public high schools jointly screen and place applicants. Students are chosen on the basis of their school attendance records, abilities, attitude, appearance, and desire for a business career. They may begin working the summer before their senior year and typically continue working 20 hours a week during the school year, usually as clerks and typists.

In 1981 Continental-Illinois Bank hired 80 percent of the students as full-time employees after graduation. An internal evaluation in 1977 found that work-study employees had a higher retention rate, a better attendance rate, and somewhat superior performance ratings than other employees at their level.

The Skills Training Education Program

The Skills Training Education Program (Project STEP) is a partnership between the Security Pacific National Bank and the 11 California Regional Occupational Programs that were established to help 72 of the state's school districts provide vocational training programs. Aimed primarily at high-school students (although some older adults are also served), Project STEP offers about 100 classes in a variety of banking skills. The courses are taught at 30 bank branches throughout the state, mostly in the Los Angeles area. Bank employees who have obtained state teaching credentials after taking a 60-hour teacher training course conduct the classes on weeknights and Saturdays and are paid by the local school districts.

Students enroll in the classes as electives on the recommendation of their advisers and receive school credit and grades. Classes range from 70 to 180 hours per semester, depending on the skills and equipment involved. Training is given to about 2,500 students each school year, at least 90 percent of whom are in high school. Security Pacific has hired at least 25 percent of the program's graduates, and other banks have hired many more. There is no formal placement assistance, but students practice filling out applications, taking clerical tests, and preparing for job interviews. Graduates receive letters of completion signed by bank vice presidents to help them. Project STEP is one of Security Pacific's Community Education Development programs, which reach 4,000 students annually. The bank also sponsors a career awareness program for children in 10 Los Angeles elementary schools. Each year about 200 students visit the main bank office to learn about opportunities and career requirements in banking. Twice annually bank employees visit junior high schools to encourage students to stay in school. Through the Exploratory Work Experience Education Program, 100 students visit bank offices each year to observe various jobs. And twice each summer 20 teachers, administrators, and counselors take part in a Summer Career and Economic Education Workshop for Educators. The workshop gives them a close look at banking careers and functions and helps them to develop a career education curriculum for their own schools.

The banking industry seems particularly well suited for collaboration with vocational education programs. Banks are present in virtually every community, the job functions vary little from one place to another, and because of high turnover rates banks often have large numbers of entry-level positions to fill. These include jobs such as teller, data entry operator, typist, clerk, stenographer, and word processor operator—all requiring skills taught in various vocational education programs.

The Philadelphia Academies

In 1969 a prototype industrial academy was started in Philadelphia for inner-city young people who could not qualify for vocational schools because they had approximately fifth-grade-level basic skills. The prototype became the Academy of Applied Electrical Sciences, directed toward students entering high school, since the greatest dropout rate occurs during the high-school years. This model three-year educational program has since given rise to three more academies—the Philadelphia Business Academy, the Academy of Applied Automotive and Mechanical Sciences, and the Philadelphia Health Academy. All are alternative schools within the Philadelphia school system, serving some 650 students.

The electrical sciences academy was conceived by a team with representatives from business and industry, labor, and education. The curriculum was designed to help students see the need to improve their reading and math abilities in order to gain specific occupational skills and thereby to motivate them to stay in school. There is also a "factory" at the academy to provide after-school and summer work experience as well as some income. The attendance rate at the academy has been 90 percent compared with 55 percent for the high schools overall, and its dropout rate has been only 1 or 2 percent compared with 30 percent overall.

The other academies have been modeled after the electrical sciences academy and supported by corporations. Each academy has a full-time director on loan from or paid by a major firm. Part-time instructors from industry and regular teachers from the schools work as a team. The program's key elements are its emphasis on the linkage between basic and vocational skills and its efforts to find jobs for the students after school and during the summer.

The Philadelphia academies' approach is now being tried in California. Many entry-level jobs were found to be going unfilled in the San Francisco area because public schools were concentrating on college-bound students and failing to prepare potential semiskilled workers for the labor market. The Peninsula Academies have been established to upgrade the basic skills of disadvantaged students while motivating them to finish high school by combining academic and vocational education with job training.

The Training Opportunities Program

A newer initiative is the Training Opportunities Program, developed by the Office of Occupational and Career Education in New York City. The purpose is to provide on-the-job training opportunities in private businesses to high-school juniors and seniors. The first-year program involved about 1,000 students, selected on the basis of interest, occupational goals, handicapping conditions, limited English-speaking ability, and interest in nontraditional careers. A total of 15 occupational clusters were identified on the basis of expanding employment needs requiring technical and heavy-equipment skills and were matched to occupational training programs in 14 participating high schools. Commitments for training slots in private industry were developed with a focus on companies with 50 or fewer employees.

Each high school selected 65-70 students who also participated in a workshop on employability skills one class period per week throughout the training period. For the first six weeks students participated in vocational exploration at the work site, during which they were paid stipends by the program equal to the minimum wage. (This period was shortened to two weeks in the 1982-1983 program.) Throughout the training period employers paid half the stipend, for a maximum of 15 hours on site a week. Firms made the final selection of students and evaluated them formally twice during the year. Trainees received vocational academic credit contingent on satisfactory ratings by their supervisors. The program was expanded in 1982 to accommodate 1,500 juniors and seniors from 25 high schools. It is funded by local taxes as well as by the employers, who contribute their facilities and equipment and pay half the stipend.

Administrative Arrangements

As Chapter 2 describes, a diversity of institutions offer vocational education programs, all with their own policies and procedures. We believe that some of these institutional characteristics affect both the quality of the programs that schools offer and the collaborative efforts that they might undertake with the private sector. In this section we discuss those characteristics and some additional administrative details independent of the schools themselves.

In their study of vocational education in large cities, Benson and Hoach-lander (1981) found that vocational programs in specialized schools (regional vocational centers or vocational high schools) were generally superior to those in comprehensive high schools. They identified five interrelated characteristics of program quality: (1) intensity of instruction, (2) attitudes and experience of teachers and counselors, (3) relationship between teachers and employers in relevant industries, (4) availability of current equipment and instructional materials, and (5) probability of graduates' finding employment with relatively high wages. Benson and Hoachlander proceeded to identify four factors that seemed to account for the higher quality of vocational programs in specialized schools: (1) greater depth of programming, offering students a full sequence of courses covering a given occupation; (2) the ability to hire and retain more experienced instructional staff, those with trade certification in some cases rather than teacher certification, and those who want to teach part-time; (3) higher priority for vocational education than in comprehensive high schools, where it is most often seen as having lower status than academic education; and (4) greater opportunity for collaboration with business and industry.

Several types of organizations already in existence can foster collaboration between vocational education and private-sector employers. Two that we discuss below are vocational education student organizations and industry-education-labor collaborative councils.

Student Organizations

There are nine major national student organizations in secondary and postsecondary vocational education, with student memberships totalling over 1.7 million in 1980-1981. The organizations recognized by the U.S. Department of Education are the

American Industrial Arts Student Association,
Distributive Education Clubs of America,
Future Business Leaders of America, Phi Beta Lamda,
Future Farmers of America,
Future Homemakers of America,
Health Occupations Students of America,
National Postsecondary Agriculture Student Organization,
Office Education Association, and
Vocational Industrial Clubs of America.

Their goals are to promote the development of vocational competencies, civic responsibility, and leadership skills in their members. These student organizations are not mandated by law, nor are they supported by public funds, but they often play an important part in the lives of vocational education students. The student organizations are supported by members' dues, donations from individuals and business and industry, and by the proceeds of projects they undertake. Some of the national organizations were formed over 50 years ago, and some local clubs are more than 70 years old.

The involvement of business, industry, and labor is an important component in these student organizations. Business and union leaders donate their time and money to them. They provide information on employment needs and education requirements. Corporate and labor leaders serve as members of their boards of directors and participate in workshops or lecture series. They also judge activities that serve as the basis of awards given to vocational club members, which are commonly used as incentives for outstanding achievement in the clubs. The clubs actively solicit employers to participate with them and encourage business, industry, and labor leaders to provide work and on-the-job training opportunities, to serve on advisory committees, and to conduct career workshops for students. In 1982, for example, the National Advisory Board of the Distributive Education Clubs of America sent a flyer to employers encouraging their involvement in vocational education. The brochure listed 57 employers (including the U.S. Armed Forces) that are actively involved with vocational education. Similar promotional activities have taken place at the state and local levels as well.

Collaborative Councils

In the late 1970s a number of local collaborative councils were formed to enhance cooperation among business and industry, labor, and education. Not all the councils have started so recently; some date back to the 1960s and one was initiated in 1947. The National Institute for Work and Learning published a directory of 150 such councils in 1981 (Gold et al., 1981). These councils have been locally initiated and depend on local leaders for their support and effectiveness. However, other broad-based groups, such as the local advisory councils for vocational education (discussed in Chapter 2), the private industry councils initiated by the federal Comprehensive Employment and Training Act and continued under the Job Training Partnership Act, and career education action councils started under the federal Career Education Incentive Act of 1977, are similar to the local collaborative councils catalogued by the National Institute for Work and Learning. Many of these broad-based councils have received widespread recognition as initiators of effective collaborative efforts between vocational education and the private sector in recent years. Councils that coordinate education and employment effectively, however, do not exist in all local areas.

Elsman reported the results of a study by the National Institute for Work and Learning (Elsman and the National Institute for Work and Learning, 1981). He observed that there is no typical pattern in the genesis of a collaborative council. They have been started by schools, chambers of commerce, businesses, other existing advisory boards, and elected officials. They are extremely diverse in their operations, their goals, and their activities as well as their beginnings. He notes that they all have broad-based membership representing more than two sectors, usually education, industry and business, labor, government, and other organizations serving young people. They are self-organized and responsible for their own continuation. They serve as neutral ground for the discussion and resolution of issues concerning members with different institutional affiliations and allegiances. Strong leadership within the council that is reflected in its dealings with the community is essential to the formation and effective functioning of a collaborative council. Some are affiliated with national groups, such as the National Work-Education Consortium or the National Association of Industry-Education Cooperation. There are also several state and regional associations of local collaborative councils.

VOCATIONAL EDUCATION AND ECONOMIC DEVELOPMENT

In Chapter 1 we described some of the changes in the nature of jobs since World War II; more recently there have been marked geographic shifts in the location of jobs. Formerly prosperous centers of industry have become economically depressed because of declines in those industries. Perhaps the most notable examples are the American automobile and steel industries, although manufacturers of many other goods—durable and nondurable—have suffered as well. Within depressed areas, the economic impact of massive layoffs or plant closings spreads to other parts of the local economy—to the places those workers would be spending their money if they were employed. In addition, declining industries are likely to curtail their training and apprenticeship programs.

In response to declining or unfavorable economic conditions, some regions of the country, all states, and some localities have adopted economic development strategies. Generally the goals are to attract new industries, revitalize existing industries, expand or diversify a state's economic base in order to increase tax revenues, and increase the employment rate for residents of the area by either retraining workers or expanding job opportunities. Some states house the administrative responsibility for economic development in a single agency, and others set up arrangments that rely on the cooperative efforts of several existing agencies. In most cases, administrators give form to their belief that a strong education and training system positively influences location decisions by including vocational education in their economic development strategies. Educators or training professionals assess employers' needs, plan training programs, develop curricula and training materials, and sometimes conduct the training programs. Employers often arrange for the education and training they need for their workers under contract with schools or local education agencies.

Economic development strategies have turned to researchers studying the creation of jobs to try to determine which firms to try to attract in order to increase employment in a locality. Birch is often cited in the economic development literature, but his work has been severely criticized (Armington and Odle, 1982). Birch concluded that small firms account for the creation of a majority of jobs in this country. He used establishment size as a proxy for firm size, thereby counting a local franchise of a national corporation, for example, as a small business. He also neglected to consider the failure rate of small businesses, which is very high and accounts for significant job loss.

A report by another committee of the National Research Council, *Rethinking Urban Policy: Urban Development in an Advanced Economy* (Hanson, 1983), presents a detailed analysis of the effects of these geographic and economic shifts on American cities. The report suggests that cities plan their economic development strategies to take advantage of their available resources. For example, in several cities the large commercial banks that had previously served primarily the locality have worked increasingly on the national and international levels. Similarly, the Boston area has for many years taken advantage of its strength in higher education institutions to attract high-technology firms and other companies that rely heavily on a highly educated work force. On a regional scale, it has been proposed that New England use its concentration of colleges and universities to attract firms, especially high-technology or research firms, as manufacturing in the area declines (Commission on Higher Education and the Economy of New England, 1982).

In 1982 the Committee for Economic Development released the results of its study of public-private partnership in seven American cities (Committee for Economic Development, 1982; Fosler and Berger, 1982). The seven cities studied, all representing purportedly successful experiences in solving urban problems, are examples of ways in which civic leaders have taken a large variety of local conditions into account, used to full advantage the strengths available, and achieved success. Local initiative supported by strong civic leaders has proved essential in all cities. In Baltimore and Chicago, for example, a political system with a strong mayor in a central role may have accounted for a portion of the success of the urban revitalization programs. The presence of large corporate headquarters favored Pittsburgh as well as Minneapolis and Saint Paul. Other factors, such as geographic location, economic base, or the age of the city, work to the advantage of other cities. However, the absence of these favorable characteristics does not imply failure in other cities. For example, Baltimore has had a declining economy and houses no major corporate headquarters but has nonetheless had some successful projects to revitalize portions of the downtown area. Education and training were by no means at the heart of the strategies of the seven cities, but they played a role in the communities' response to economic and employment conditions.

In 1981 the American Vocational Association published a handbook for vocational educators to use in assisting with economic development strategies (Paul and Carlos, 1981). In preparing the book, the authors visited 17 sites with active economic development projects involving vocational educators. From the diversity of activities they encountered they extracted guidelines for vocational educators to use in working with economic development and industry personnel. The varied functions of a "linking agent," a person coordinating the activities of educators and business people, are described. The handbook also gives instructions on how to plan industry training programs and how to secure funding and technical assistance for economic development activities.

Bushnell (1980) stressed the importance of vocational education in economic development activities. His paper has a decidedly optimistic tone; he notes the numerous examples of active involvement of vocational educators in planning and implementing such state and local programs. However, a position statement of the National Association of State Directors of Vocational Education (1981:4) offers a slightly different perspective, noting:

The role of vocational education in economic development is not mentioned in federal legislation [on vocational education]. It is not included in most state plans for vocational education. It cannot be found in the annals of accomplishments of vocational education. Even the dramatic accomplishments in economic development documented for some vocational education programs go unnoticed and unheralded by the national leadership.

The document suggests ways in which vocational educators should improve program offerings and assert themselves in order to play a more active role in economic development. Taken together, these two documents (Bushnell, 1980; National Association of State Directors of Vocational Education, 1981) suggest that in many cases the involvement of vocational educators in economic development activities may have been less the result of their own assertive efforts than recognition by others of the importance of a strong education and training system closely tied with businesses. While some vocational educators have initiated an active role in economic development efforts, many have not. Opportunities exist for more vocational educators to become actively involved in economic development efforts.

CONCLUSION

There is enormous variety in the types of activities that schools and businesses can collaborate to accomplish and in the arrangements they choose for doing so. The success of vocational education programs and their collaborative elements depends in large measure on their ability to respond and adapt to the changing economy and to local situations. In addition, federal and state laws and regulations, such as those regarding certification of teachers or corporate taxes, can positively affect vocational education programs and facilitate collaborative efforts.

4 Strengthening Vocational Education: Conclusions and Recommendations

VOCATIONAL EDUCATION AND THE CHANGING ECONOMY

Human capital is this country's greatest natural resource. At a time when many newly industrializing countries are upgrading the capabilities of their peoples at an unprecedented rate and when older industrial nations, now fully recovered from the effects of World War II, are challenging the technological predominance of the United States, the qualities and capacities of the American work force cannot be allowed to deteriorate. In this chapter we call on the nation's public education system to do its part to strengthen the U.S. economy and its position in the world economy. We present conclusions and recommendations derived from our analysis of the material in the preceding chapters.

Underlying our analysis and recommendations is the belief that vocational education has characteristics that distinguish it from other kinds of education in fundamental and important ways. Vocational programs are often conducted in settings different from those of academic or general education. Vocational education teachers frequently gain their occupational training and experience in industry, not in schools of education, as do most academic or general education teachers. The funding requirements of vocational programs may well be different from those of other programs. Our recommendations derive from these and other distinctive characteristics of vocational education and are intended to accommodate and to use to advantage these differences.

We believe that vocational education suffers from being conferred generally lower status than academic education, particularly at the high-school level. The status problem affects vocational education at the federal level, in state governments, and in the administration of vocational programs in local school districts. The detrimental effects of this inferior status are nowhere more apparent than in comprehensive high schools everywhere, in which vocational education is often overlooked or slighted in favor of college preparatory education. Some of the problems are overcome in special vocational high schools and postsecondary vocational programs, in which many programs are of relatively high quality and their status is generally higher and more conducive to effective operations. All of our recommendations are intended to improve the quality of vocational education programs and thereby to begin to raise their status.

As we saw in Chapter 1, the challenges to vocational education posed by a changing world economy are complex and numerous. New entrants into the labor force require a level and range of skills different from those needed by past generations. Older workers in fading industries must develop new skills or accept lower wages, sometimes both. Productive members of society will increasingly be expected to modify, upgrade, and update their knowledge and skills in response to a pace of technological change at least as rapid as occurred during the great industrialization of America a century ago.

The proportion of the American work force employed in manufacturing occupations has been declining for nearly four decades, and employment growth has been concentrated in service jobs. While there is disagreement as to the future growth in output of the manufacturing sector in the United States, there is agreement that employment opportunities in manufacturing industries will not increase. Any growth in manufacturing output will be due to the adoption of a more capital-intensive technology. As a consequence, not only will there be fewer jobs in manufacturing in the future, but also those that exist are likely to require different skills than are needed today. Moreover, the skills necessary for the service, financial, and other growth sectors are obviously different from those traditionally necessary in manufacturing. The problem of designing vocational education programs to meet these changing skill requirements is that there is no agreement on what these skill requirements will be or even on the general direction of change.

The precise direction this change will take is even more difficult to specify. For example, while it is clear that the revolution in information processing has just begun, we cannot predict precisely the range of applications, the speed with which they will be adopted, and the skills that workers will need in the new industries that this revolution is generating. Given the uncertainty regarding the skill requirements of the economy, it is essential that the education of America's young people is designed to enhance their abilities to adapt as necessary to these changing requirements.

When change is rapid and its precise direction is difficult to predict, institutions that must adapt to these changes should be flexible. They require multiple channels through which information about economic, technological, and educational change can be processed. The decision points regarding how and when to implement change should be as decentralized as feasible, but local administrators or decision makers need information from national and state levels. Adaptation at the local level can be encouraged through the supply of sufficient information for decision making. Decentralization allows for flexibility and adaptation in some parts of the system, even if others remain sluggish and slow to respond.

As Chapter 2 noted, vocational education institutions in the United States on the whole are highly varied, contain an extraordinary range of points of decision, and have a considerable capacity to adapt to change. Just to name the types of vocational educational institutions is to emphasize their diversity. Vocational programs in comprehensive high schools are perhaps the most numerous and best known. At this level there are also specialized vocational high schools, regional technical institutes, and area vocational centers, which high-school students attend on a part-time basis.

Postsecondary vocational education is even more varied and complex. Junior and community colleges provide an extensive, varied, and highly flexible set of vocational programs. In addition, there are proprietary schools; regional occupational centers; on-the-job training provided directly by industry, CETA, or JTPA centers; trade schools; and apprenticeship programs.

The mix of these institutions and their mode of operation vary greatly among states and among regions within states. In some parts of the country, postsecondary schools play the dominant public role. In other states, regional technical schools are key. In still others, specialized vocational high schools make especially valuable contributions.

While some policy analysts may object to the variety and overlapping responsibilities of vocational education institutions, the committee believes that the complexity of the system contributes to its strength. To the extent that vocational programs compete with one another for students, for teachers, for public resources, and for contacts with local business and industry, these institutions have incentives to modify and adapt their training to the changing labor market. The revolution in word and data processing, for example, has generated a strong market demand for workers with skills relevant to the operation of computers. Actions to supply training programs came first from industry. Postsecondary schools and proprietary institutions and now the more advanced high-school programs are upgrading their offerings in these areas. Those parts of the country in which program innovation was most rapid are reaping the economic advantages. Other states and localities are now making their own assiduous efforts to catch up, usually through state or regional economic development plans. Even though sluggishness may be found in some places, it is doubtful that a more centrally planned vocational education system would have responded to technological change more quickly.

As decentralized and flexible as the American vocational educational system is, however, many of its components have become rigid and stagnant, and it is in these areas that institutional reform is especially needed. The greatest problems are found at the secondary level, particularly in comprehensive high schools. Here public vocational education across the country began some six or seven decades ago, and here past practices have become so deeply embedded in an institutional framework that flexibility and responsiveness are more the exception than the rule. Requirements governing the recruitment, certification, promotion, compensation, and retention of teachers are so well defined that adaptation to new technologies is costly and slow. Also problematic are rules governing the allocation of resources, the acquisition of equipment, and the use of facilities.

The Role of Vocational Education in Economic Development

In economic terms, vocational education can be viewed as an investment in human capital to the extent that it contributes to the future earnings (and thereby increases the productivity) of its graduates who are employed. Some people enroll in vocational education programs while they are working in order to upgrade their skills, thus increasing their productivity and attractiveness to their employers. Other students, particularly those in high school, are not working in jobs they will continue to hold after they graduate and will look for jobs once they graduate from school. Obviously, vocational education programs can improve the job productivity of their students only if there are ultimately job openings for those students to fill. Therefore, a healthy local economy clearly increases the returns to vocational education programs.

But can vocational education programs actually create a healthy local economy? While it is true that strong economies have skilled work forces, that firms consistently rate the presence of a skilled work force as an important determinant of their location decisions, and that vocational education programs increase the skill levels of their students, it does not follow that vocational education programs can create a pool of skilled labor in an economically depressed area. Because the skilled graduates of vocational education programs most often leave distressed areas that cannot provide employment opportunities, a skilled labor pool cannot be developed and kept in place for any period of time. A strong vocational education program can nonetheless be an important component in local economic development initiatives. If a local vocational education program has the capacity to provide the training required by particular employers considering an area for relocation, the vocational education program itself can be a strong force in attracting them. It is the capacity of the program to meet or adapt to specific needs of employers, not the number of students trained or the pool created, that has the potential to attract jobs.

Responsibilities of the Public Education System

We have noted the critical need for young adults to master the basic educational skills and work habits required to achieve employability, whether college bound or not, and to attain more specific vocational skills and experiences. We also have noted that far too many high-school graduates are deficient in basic or vocational skills, work habits, or all of these. The complex array of individual, family, and community factors that contribute to such socially unwanted results notwithstanding, we believe that the public education system must take responsibility for ensuring that young people are effectively prepared for both employment and further education. Every young person must be prepared, upon graduation from high school, for employment, further study, or both. All too often preparation of college-bound high-school students has in the practices of high schools taken precedence over preparation for employment, with the unhappy result that vocational education students have inadequate basic and occupational skills. We believe that providing an effective array of vocational education opportunities is a role of public high schools equal in importance to their role of preparing students for college.

While we do recommend expanded efforts at collaboration between vocational education and the private sector, we do not believe that employers should assume greatly increased responsibility for education and training. The economics of the private sector would work against employers assuming major responsibility for educating and training their employees. Probably only large firms could afford to do a substantial amount of training. Once trained, the workers would become a marketable commodity; firms would compete to hire them. The trained employees would be hired away from the firms that paid for the training, thus eventually removing their incentive to train. This situation is full justification for keeping the responsibility for employment training or vocational education in the public sector, where it is now.

The diversity of educational institutions, which we support in general, makes it all too easy for each school or program to avoid assuming the responsibility for ensuring that students have adequate grounding in basic and vocational skills. Paradoxically, the fragmentation seems most severe in comprehensive high schools, which house academic, general, and vocational education programs. The teaching of basic educational skills is problematic both because of their importance and because of the ill-defined nature of the responsibility for teaching them. Vocational education teachers and administrators can shift the responsibility for failing to teach students who are not competent in the basic skills to other parts of the school system; in fact, teachers of academic and general education most often have not wanted vocational teachers to assume responsibility for teaching basic educational skills.

The primary responsibility for teaching basic skills should be borne by elementary-school teachers and administrators. Introducing occupational information in the elementary grades can, we believe, help to motivate some students who are otherwise uninterested in learning school subjects. Remediation at the high-school level is a more difficult problem, one that often has ill-defined responsibilities. Issues to be resolved include who should bear the costs of remediation in high schools, how to motivate students, and which teachers are the best equipped to teach basic skills at this level.

VOCATIONAL EDUCATION AND THE PRIVATE SECTOR

As we have seen, collaboration between educators and business or labor leaders is not a new idea. The Vocational Education Act of 1963 established the policy of involving the private sector in vocational education planning through national, state, and local advisory councils. Employers and unions have been involved in the activities of vocational student organizations for many years. There are national organizations for people who carry out collaborative activities, such as the National Association of Industry-Education Cooperation and the National Work-Education Consortium. Close ties with business and labor seem to be typical of high-quality vocational education programs. The committee believes that collaboration between education and employment is needed in far more settings. We believe that collaborative ventures should be extended to other programs and situations and that a wide variety of options is open to those who want to improve their vocational programs through collaboration with employers.

Why should businesses use their resources to help public schools prepare students for work? When most businesses are dealing with difficult economic conditions, incentives to collaborate with schools must include more than an appeal to their sense of civic responsibility. Collaborative efforts must be demonstrated to be advantageous to them.

The availability of a trained work force may prove incentive enough to firms that otherwise would have difficulty hiring qualified workers. Thus it is rather easy to see why there are already links between such employers and high-quality vocational education programs. In such situations collaboration works to the advantage of all involved. However, using collaborative efforts to improve weak programs may require that educators be induced to improve their programs and change their administative procedures and that businesses be induced to use their resources to help improve the qualifications of program graduates.

The benefits of collaborative efforts accrue principally to employers, who gain access to better-trained potential employees, and to students, who receive better training and occupational experience. Schools benefit in that they can provide better training. Teachers benefit if they receive training or work experience from private-sector employers. Insofar as collaboration improves the education and training of future workers, it benefits society by increasing the workers' productivity and enhancing economic growth.

Education and training are improved by collaboration with private-sector employers in four ways. First, with aid from the private sector, schools can gain access to better, up-to-date equipment and can then modify their curricula accordingly in order to train students in up-to-date job skills. Second, through collaboration and the sharing of information, schools can prepare students for jobs that are likely to be available when the students graduate. Third, students who have contact with employers through their school programs are likely to develop positive work habits and may find it easier to get jobs once they graduate. Fourth, through their supervised work experiences, students establish an employment record that may help them get jobs.

Characteristics of Successful Collaborative Efforts

Most successful collaborative efforts are initiated locally, but some are organized at the state or regional (within the state) level, and some successful local ventures expand to the state or even the national level. The types of projects that are successful in local situations vary greatly. Collaborative efforts are created in response to a perceived local need or problem. What works in Boston may fail in Houston. And a work-study arrangement that is effective for the Continental-Illinois Bank in Chicago may not work for a graphics firm in the same city. From this enormous diversity we can draw generalizations based on studies of collaborative projects that have been judged successful.

Collaborative projects are like any other human endeavor in that their success depends on the individuals involved. The personal commitment of top leaders on all sides is critical. And, of course, the competence of the people actually running the project is essential. The best way to initiate and sustain a collaborative project may be through a "catalytic agent," that is, one key individual who is committed to the project, who can effectively communicate with the essential parties on all sides, who has a sense of what will generate success and what will fail. The catalytic agent may come from the school, from the business firm, from a labor union, or from a community-based organization, but he or she must understand the roles of all in the joint effort. Collaborative ventures, by their very nature, are voluntary and will be effective only if all the individuals involved are committed to the endeavor and are active, contributing participants. In such projects there are only active participants; none of the principal parties serves in a purely advisory role.

The locus of the initiative for any particular project does not determine its success or failure; schools and businesses are equally likely to start success-ful partnerships. Some projects involve only one program or school and one business firm, perhaps also with the participation of a labor union or a community-based organization. A vocational education program may, for example, modify slightly its curriculum to adapt to advances in an occupa-tion with the assistance of industry in the form of borrowed equipment, borrowed personnel, supervised work experience for students, or summer internships for teachers. In other instances, several firms needing employ-ees with the same general skills may band together to work with several schools in a district. The impetus for either type of project may come from any one of the participants. Reviews of collaborative efforts reveal that most start on a rather modest scale, perhaps involving only one vocational program or a few student workers. Once the project is under way, opera-tions can be modified as necessary, and the endeavor can be expanded. Frequently employers who have once worked with the schools seek further involvement, perhaps in new areas such as basic skills or in elementary schools when they had previously worked exclusively with high-school vocational education students.

Some people believe it is easier to sell collaborative projects, that is, to gain continued or increased support or to initiate such an effort in a new setting, if their success can be demonstrated. Documentation may be facilitated if the goals of the undertaking are clearly stated and if modest but usable records of progress toward meeting those goals are maintained. In this way, all concerned parties—business people, educators, labor leaders, community leaders, students, and parents—can judge the value of the projects.

We have noted before that there are many examples of successful collaborative efforts, but many more are needed. Why have they not arisen spontaneously? Some require relatively small investments of money or equipment, but all require a sizable investment of people's time and energy. Public-school teachers or administrators are logical ones to reach out to business for assistance in various forms, but they are exceedingly busy, sometimes overburdened, with the daily work of operating their programs or schools. Sometimes, too, school personnel do not know how to make contact with employers in the private sector. Community-based organizations, labor unions, or employers themselves could assist in such instances. Presumably, when enough vocational education teachers gain work experience in industry, this barrier can be overcome more easily.

Attitudes toward education and training are also critical to collaboration. Educators must acknowledge that they do not have a monopoly on teaching and that the traditional arrangements of teaching may need to be altered to suit the needs of students, employers, and educators. Students and workers should look forward to periodic retraining throughout their working lives. Education should be viewed as an open process, one that encompasses all of a person's life, not just the hours spent in school and not just the school years.

Legislation has been proposed in the U.S. Senate that would offer tax incentives to corporations to encourage them to contribute equipment and other forms of support to schools. One such bill, S. 1195, the High Technology Research and Educational Development Act of 1983, would include secondary and postsecondary vocational schools as well as elementary schools in its provisions. Corporate contributions that would carry tax advantages ("enhanced deductions") include computer equipment, software, and related orientation, maintenance, and repair services; scientific and technical equipment not more than three years old for use in education, research, and research training; and financial supplementation of faculty salaries or the loan of instructors from business and industry personnel.

Recommendations

Collaboration with Employers   Mechanisms and incentives should be established to induce educators and employers to work together in the planning and provision of occupational education and training. Incentives for teachers could include releasing them from teaching and administrative duties, giving bonuses for establishing links with private-sector employers, and awarding internships in business. Education administrators should give consideration to awarding school credit to students who take courses taught in collaboration with employers—in the workplace or by corporate personnel. Tax incentives may be appropriate to encourage firms to donate equipment to schools and to allow schools to use the employers' equipment for training purposes in the workplace. The equipment used for training need not always be new, but it should not be obsolete. Tax incentives may also be used to encourage employers to lend personnel to teach or to help support vocational education teachers in the schools.

Coordination of Vocational Education and Employment Training   There should be as much overlap as feasible in membership on local vocational education councils and private industry councils and on the state vocational education advisory committees and the state coordinating councils required by the Job Training Partnership Act. The committee endorses the provisions of the JTPA intended to ensure coordination among employment training organizations and the public school system.

In urging better coordination between JTPA and public vocational education, we do not wish to remove all apparent redundancy. As noted at the beginning of this chapter, we believe that a diverse and decentralized system can better serve individuals' educational needs and respond more quickly to changes in the economy than could a monolithic education system. We recommend coordination in order to ensure the existence of an appropriate array of schools and training centers with different approaches necessary to meet the educational and training objectives of a diverse population.

Supervised Work Experience for Students

As we described in Chapter 2, there are three main types of work-experience programs in which vocational education students can participate: cooperative education, work-study, and apprenticeship programs. While each of these tends to have distinctive characteristics, good programs share certain traits. The following comments apply least of all to work-study programs, however, since their primary purpose is to give economically disadvantaged students paid employment rather than work experience as an adjunct to training.

The two components of any supervised work-experience program—the education and the employment—should be closely related to one another. This principle is obvious, but it is not always followed. The importance and relevance of the skills taught in school should be made evident to the students both while they are in school and while they are working. Likewise, the work required of the students on the job should be as close as possible to that required once the training program is completed, that is, in regular full-time jobs.

The best programs with work-experience components are ones in which completion is determined on the basis of mastery of certain knowledge and skills, not simply on the passage of time. The objectives of the training and the work should be clearly stated before students enroll in the programs. Progression toward competency in both components of the program should be determined at reasonable intervals throughout the program.

The work-experience component of the program should be carefully supervised by the employer and also by a teacher or coordinator from the school. While this is standard practice in high-quality programs, it is not universally done. By saying that teachers or education coordinators should monitor the work of students, we do not mean that school personnel should be given authority over employees in the workplace. They should visit the students on the job periodically to see the work conditions, the work assignments, the type and extent of supervision, the nature of contact with other employees, and the like. This coordination by school personnel is essential to the meshing of the components of the program and also to the assignment of school credit for the work portion of the program when it is applicable.

Wherever feasible the employers and education coordinators should make arrangements that enable students to work alongside other employees so that they see what full-time paid employment is really like. In this way, the students have the best opportunity to observe practical and effective work habits. It is important for them to see which of their habits or expectations are at variance with the behavior employers wish to see in their employees. In some industrial settings it may not be possible for students to be totally integrated with the regular work force. Concerns for security or occupational safety or constraints imposed by the students' limited skills may militate against their being incorporated into the regular work environment. In such cases, and we hope they are few, extra efforts should be made to give the students routine exposure, albeit on a limited basis, to regular employees and their work.

Remediation of deficiencies in basic educational skills should be separate from the work experience. It is not reasonable to expect employers to remedy these deficiencies or to employ students seriously in need of educational remediation. However, the schools can and should provide remediation to students who need help in mastering the basic skills before they participate in work-experience programs. Lack of competence in the basic skills contributes to the problem of access to high-quality vocational programs, which is discussed later in this chapter. The committee believes that to burden the employment component of such programs with remediation is to doom them to failure. Similarly, to expect employers to hire students who have not mastered the basic educational and occupational skills required on the job is unrealistic; employers must be allowed to set reasonable criteria for selecting students for work-experience programs.

Recommendations

Competency-Based Work-Experience Programs   Unions, educators, and employers should work to change the requirements for the completion of cooperative education and apprenticeship programs; they should be based on competence rather than time. This change will be fraught with difficulties and will require the expenditure of considerable money and time, but we believe it is extremely important. Currently the most common arrangement requires that people participate in apprenticeship programs for a specified period of time, after which they become journeymen. In cooperative education programs, high-school graduation signifies completion. Some unions are working to modify apprenticeship systems, but progress is slowed by competing demands for the personnel and financial resources necessary to make the required changes. The difficulties in trying to revise programs along these lines are analogous to those in instituting minimum competency tests as the basis for awarding high-school diplomas. The difficulties in deciding what competencies should be included, deciding what levels of skill are required, and determining how to measure these abilities are not to be underestimated.

Apprenticeship Programs   The Office of Vocational and Adult Education in the U.S. Department of Education should work with the Federal Committee on Apprenticeship and the Bureau of Apprenticeship Training in the U.S. Department of Labor to revise the criteria for completion of apprenticeship programs. Completion should be based on competence rather than the period of participation in the programs. These groups should take the lead in developing appropriate training curricula and competency tests for apprenticeship programs. The Department of Labor should fund work by unions to develop criteria for completion and competency tests.

IMPROVING VOCATIONAL EDUCATION PROGRAMS

We have identified three main areas in which we think public vocational education needs improvement. Our general approach is to recommend methods or policies that work in some settings and to apply them to the institution with the greatest need for improvement—public comprehensive high schools.

Our first concern is vocational education teachers, particularly at the high-school level. We recommend changes in their pre-service and in-service training, in their certification, and in the policies governing their hiring and pay. Our second concern is the funding of public vocational education programs. We highlight problems and make recommendations based on our collective experience about what works in other situations.

Our third concern is access to high-quality vocational education programs, particularly for economically or educationally disadvantaged students. In this case we take a different tack. A significant part of the problem is the deficiencies in basic educational or occupational skills or work habits of disadvantaged students. We believe it would do no good for us simply to recommend stronger basic education and more effective socialization of these students. Therefore, we have chosen to recommend experimentation with a radically different way of improving access to programs and also remedying deficiencies in the basic skills of students. We acknowledge that our approach will meet with immediate and strong opposition from some quarters. We are willing to take the risk since more conventional means have not proved effective. We want to urge, however, that these particular recommendations be used to supplement and not to supplant current efforts in remediation and improving access. In other words, the funding of regular programs should continue at no less than the current levels and should not be diminished by experimentation.

Strengthening Teaching

The primary place of training and certification of vocational education teachers is in colleges of education, which seem to operate primarily to prepare teachers of academic subjects. By and large they have not paid special attention to vocational education and the differences in teaching methods required for vocational in contrast to other education. Occupational experience in industry, which can be extremely valuable for those who teach vocational skills, is often not awarded college credit, nor is it considered in the certification process.

Certification requirements are set at the state or local level, so there is variation across the country. Public-high-school teachers—vocational and other—are usually required to hold teachers' certificates earned through work at teachers' colleges. Certification requirements often specify particular courses or particular teacher training institutions—requirements that reduce flexibility in hiring and eliminate the possibility of discovering whether other types of preparation are effective. Requirements are not as stringent at the postsecondary level, so administrators have more flexibility and a potentially larger pool of teachers from which to choose. The single most important difference in vocational education at the two levels is that postsecondary schools can hire people who have gained their occupational training in business rather than in the classroom. This is generally viewed as an option that should be available to high schools, a view that the committee shares.

The committee is not convinced that the benefits of certification requirements for vocational education teachers outweigh the costs. We do know that the requirements limit the pool of potential teachers, some of whom might be talented and effective. We believe there should be university-based training for teachers, but we believe that allowance should be made for other types of training, particularly occupational training or experience in the workplace.

We believe that the best way of determining the most effective means of preparing teachers is to let education administrators choose those people who appear to have the requisite occupational and teaching skills. Administrators' choices will be made harder and riskier because of the difficulty in trying to predict who will be effective teachers. Such choice currently exists at the postsecondary but not generally at the secondary level. Nevertheless, we believe the risk is worth taking, at least on a trial basis, in order to improve the preparedness of vocational education teachers. If administrators select teachers who have no formal training in teaching, they should provide and require in-service training in these skills. Taken together, these provisions would allow greater flexibility in hiring teachers while giving some insurance against potentially harmful deficiencies in teaching abilities.

Awarding tenure to teachers is often thought to remove some of their incentives to adapt to change. This is of particular concern for vocational education, given the constantly and rapidly changing world of work to which vocational programs must adapt. The problem of keeping programs current is especially severe at the high-school level, in large measure because of the high proportion of tenured high-school teachers. Seniority, especially as a factor in deciding who is fired in a reduction in the teaching force, contributes to the problem of keeping vocational education teachers current in their occupational fields.

Pay structures for high-school teachers—vocational or other—generally do not differentiate pay levels by field or competence. This makes it extremely difficult for schools to attract and retain teachers in subjects that are in high demand (such as computer-related or technical fields) or to reward especially effective teachers. While there has been widespread and vehement resistance to changing pay scales, experiments or new policies are being instituted in several places across the country.

The level of teachers' salaries is an extremely sensitive issue. As noted at a convocation on precollege science and mathematics education held at the National Academy of Sciences (National Academy of Sciences and National Academy of Engineering, 1982), opinions vary about how to raise the quality of high-school teachers. Some think pay for all teachers is too low to attract qualified people. Others think differential pay should be instituted so that market forces can work to adjust the salaries of teachers. Houston and Memphis are experimenting with differential pay scales, but the projects are still under way and the effects of the experiments have not been determined. Others think that low morale is a more severe problem than low pay and that recognition for outstanding performance and freedom from noninstructional duties would improve the quality of teaching.

Recommendations

Certification of Teachers   Requirements for the certification of vocational education teachers should be modified to reflect the needs of vocational education—in particular, the importance of occupational training or experience in industry. Certification should be based on judged competence in both teaching and the relevant occupation rather than on completion of a bachelor's degree in teacher education, which may be largely irrelevant to vocational education programs.

Training of Teachers   To serve adequately the needs of vocational education, teacher training institutions should develop, in addition to the standard curriculum, special curricula for people who have gained most of their occupational knowledge and experience through employment and not in college. The curricula for vocational education teachers should be short, effective, and aimed at teaching practices in a wider variety of instructional settings than curricula in many other education programs. They should allow people trained in the workplace to demonstrate their occupational skills and be exempted from some occupational courses.

In-Service Training of Teachers   In-service training programs for vocational education teachers should offer a variety of opportunities for teachers with different strengths and weaknesses. Effectiveness in teaching should be stressed for those teachers (most often those who learned their occupational skills in industry) who have little experience in teaching. Internships in business should be made available on a regular basis so that all vocational education teachers can periodically sharpen their occupational skills and knowledge. Such work experience should be considered part of in-service training for teachers and should be awarded appropriate credit in a system that requires such.

Part-Time Vocational Education Teachers   Once certification requirements are changed appropriately, high-school administrators should take advantage of opportunities to hire part-time teachers for vocational education programs. Recruitment efforts should be focused on employees in the private sector who are competent both in their occupations and in instructing others in their areas of expertise. This practice has been effective in postsecondary institutions, and we believe it could be used to ease the problems in high schools as well.

Pay Scales for Teachers   Pay systems that reward the excellence of individual teachers and permit differentiation by field should be instituted wherever possible. Such arrangements should be included in collective bargaining agreeements.

Strengthening Financing

For funding purposes vocational education might well be viewed as more similar to university research programs than to other secondary education. Vocational program costs are highly variable and depend on equipment costs to a greater degree than many academic programs. The costs of keeping programs current with changing technology and of initiating new programs in reponse to the demands of the economy often exceed available funds. These costs for any program, while not incurred annually, need to be accommodated by the annual budgets of local and state education agencies.

As we have seen, capitation financing formulas for school programs limit the ability of education administrators to allocate funds according to changing priorities or differences in program costs. Capitation funding is a disincentive to schools' allowing students to attend classes in other schools.

Funds available to accommodate changing priorities within vocational education and to improve or update programs are limited. The problem is particularly acute at local levels, where programs are modified and collaboration with the private sector is undertaken. Funds for program improvement tend to be spread thinly over many purposes, with little opportunity to assemble a critical mass of funds to achieve needed change in any one area.

Finding funds to purchase or lease expensive capital equipment is often difficult, especially in local school districts, and arrangements to exploit fully the available equipment among different programs or schools are sometimes difficult to implement. The need for expensive equipment is often short term, offering the opportunity for several programs or schools to use the same equipment if barriers to sharing can be overcome.

Recommendations

Funding Formulas In addition to enrollment figures, vocational education program funding formulas should include factors that reflect determinants of program cost, such as the educational disadvantage of students (requiring remediation), the costs of capital equipment, the salaries of teachers and administrators, curriculum revision, and the like. Formulas should permit a phased shift in funding for students who are jointly enrolled in two schools or who shift from one school to another.

Pooling Equipment Statewide and regional pools of expensive equipment that reasonably can be shared should be established. At the local level capital equipment resources, both public and private, should be identified, and means for scheduling their use among several programs should be established. Opportunities for leasing equipment, particularly for short-term training programs or economic development efforts, should be investigated. Similarly, opportunities for borrowing equipment from businesses should be sought.

Funding for Program Improvement If public schools are to accomplish the goal of providing up-to-date and effective vocational education for all students who want it, they should have sufficient resources not only to maintain the good programs they have now but also to modify existing programs and initiate new ones to teach the skills required by employers. They will also need additional money to provide remediation for educationally disadvantaged students.

Improving Access to Vocational Education Programs

Young people who live in economically depressed rural areas or inner cities frequently find it difficult to gain access to high-quality education and training programs. Where high-quality programs are available, students with deficiencies in basic skills may be denied access because there are more qualified applicants than places in the programs. In such cases, there is virtually no incentive for schools to provide remediation for the basic skills deficiencies of the students who apply for admission to the programs. Administrators of superior programs have little incentive to seek out inner-city or rural young people as students or to help them meet quickly the academic requirements of admission.

A second barrier to enrollment for disadvantaged students is the simple undersupply of sound vocational programs in many but by no means all depressed inner-city or rural communities. There may be few high-quality programs that are located within commuting distance of inner-city or rural residents. If economically disadvantaged young people from these areas move to an area in which there are better training opportunities, they generally do not have the financial resources necessary to enroll in the better programs.

The committee has considered two plans, which seem to merit experimentation, designed to ameliorate the problem of access to high-quality vocational education programs. The first is a system of vocational incentive grants, patterned after basic education opportunity grants. Such a system would provide grants to institutions on behalf of students between the ages of 14 and 18. The size of the grant would be scaled to the student's economic resources, generally including family income and economic obligations. The grants could be used to obtain vocational training in public or private schools anywhere in the country, without regard to the previous residence of the student. The grants would provide for training for each eligible student at maximum value equal to 100-120 percent of national average expenditures per student in secondary vocational education programs. Students could use their grants any time during their four years of eligibility and for sufficient time to complete their programs.

We believe that such a program would encourage the development of good training programs in geographic areas inhabited by low-income families. The funding mechanism would provide a stronger incentive than currently exists for training institutions to enroll low-income youth. Such a program should supplement existing programs and efforts to improve access. The amount paid to an institution would be independent of other resources—public or private—available to the accredited institution. Public vocational schools would have some advantage in competition with private schools because they would receive not only the vocational incentive grants but also the usual public funds. We have deliberately suggested a relatively high maximum amount for each grant to ensure adequate attention to basic skills as well as to vocational education needs. A vocational incentive grant program could give low-income students a larger choice in vocational programs than they currently have.

The second model is adapted from the approach now used to design education programs for students with handicapping conditions. Under this arrangement state and local education agencies would be required to develop an individualized vocational education plan for every high-school student who sought it for any of the standard program offerings. The plan would specify objectives for both basic skills and vocational education as well as the programs through which the objectives could be met. To the extent that the objectives could not be met by the local public school, arrangements could be made with the active assistance and oversight of the state agency to make use of any appropriate resources—public or private, local or other—to meet those objectives. Federal, state, and local resources that ordinarily could be used for the education of the student could be applied to meeting the plan objectives, and the local and state agencies would be accountable for the quality and appropriateness of the vocational education provided.

The primary advantages of this approach lie in the required focus on the needs of individual students, the increased potential for recognizing problems and assigning responsibility, the increased participation of relevant people in the education decisions, and the potential use of community-wide resources to fulfill objectives. The primary disadvantages lie in the substantially increased cost, especially in human resources, of preparing the plans; the disincentives to enroll more students, since they may request such plans; and the relatively weak incentives to create new program opportunities.

The committee recognizes that these two approaches—vocational incentive grants and individualized vocational education plans—represent significant departures from current practices and is therefore unwilling to recommend national implementation of either model without substantial empirical study. We have far more confidence in the practicality and effectiveness of vocational incentive grants, however, and frame our recommendations accordingly. We know that such grants are likely to meet with strenuous opposition within the education community. Still, we believe experimentation is warranted and should help to improve vocational education programs and disadvantaged students' access to better programs.

An important and anticipated effect of vocational incentive grants is the promotion of competition and entrepreneurship in the provision of vocational education. Private and public schools alike would compete to enroll students, presumably by strengthening their programs and by actively recruiting to enroll students with such grants. This open competition offers the advantage of flexibility, but it also raises the issue of consumer protection. Students should not unknowingly waste their grants and their time on ineffective training programs. Two procedures could avoid this: One is accreditation of training institutions, and the other is a requirement for "truth in training." Truth in training, as outlined in our recommendation below, is the less cumbersome procedure and, if carried out effectively, is likely to provide a greater degree of protection overall. It would be relatively easy to implement, since vocational educators are accustomed to evaluating their programs in terms of completions and placements of students and in terms of employers' views of training. The two procedures are not mutually incompatible and could well be used jointly.

For programs that have been in existence three or more years, the truth-in-training evaluation should include data on enrollments, completions, placements, and beginning wages. The academic qualifications of program completers should be described. A forecast of job openings for the next two years should be given. Upon request, potential applicants should be given the name, address, and telephone number of the personnel office of firms that have hired graduates. For newer programs, the materials provided to prospective students should include as much of the above information as possible, together with a somewhat more thorough prospectus describing the skills to be taught, the types of training and work experience, the expected size of the job market, minimum academic qualifications required of students, and the training and experience of faculty.

Recommendations

Vocational Incentive Grants   The federal government should initiate a substantial experiment in vocational incentive grants for high-school vocational education students. The experiment should be designed to test eligibility criteria, appropriate grant levels, and implementation processes and to assess the effects on students and educational institutions. The purposes and authorities of the Job Training Partnership Act seem appropriate to this experiment, and the resources therein, together with those available to the U.S. Department of Education, should be used to finance this work.

Consumer Protection in Vocational Education   All training institutions that accept vocational incentive grants or that receive Vocational Education Act funds should be required to provide to any interested party detailed descriptions of their programs, including courses offered, skills taught, requirements for enrollment, and opportunities for work experience, as well as written evaluations of each of their programs.

CONCLUSION

In this chapter we have outlined our findings and conclusions regarding the vocational education system, its relation to the changing economy, its role in economic development, its interaction with private-sector employers, and its institutional strengths and weaknesses. Readers who would like to place a vastly increased responsibility for training on employers will be disappointed with our recommendations. We firmly believe that it is the responsibility of the public education system to prepare students for both employment and further education. We do not think that responsibility should be shifted to private employers, although we do think employers can help significantly in the ways we have outlined.

We believe that some important and fundamental changes need to be made in the vocational education system if it is to do its job effectively. Probably the most important of those changes are intended to strengthen the teaching and financing of vocational education. One central change that we see as desirable seems virtually impossible to legislate or institute. We would like to see vocational education become an equal partner with college-preparatory education in the education system as a whole. The most effective vocational programs are deserving of that respect now, and we would like to see all programs raised to that level of quality and esteem.

References

Armington, Catherine, and Marjorie Odle
  1982   Small Business—how many jobs? *The Brookings Review* 1(2):14-17.
Ayers, Robert, and Steven Miller
  1981   The Impacts of Industrial Robots. Report number CMU-RI-TR 81-7. The Robotics Institute, Department of Engineering and Public Policy, Carnegie-Mellon University.
Bassi, Laurie J.
  1982   *The Effect of CETA on Participants' Post-Program Earnings.* Washington, D.C.: The Urban Institute.
Bell, Terrell H., and Kenneth B. Hoyt
  1974   *Career Education: The USOE Perspective.* Occasional Paper No. 4. Columbus, Ohio: The Center for Vocational Education, Ohio State University.
Bendick, Marc
  1982   Employment, training and economic development. In John L. Palmer and Isabel V. Sawhill, eds., *The Reagan Experiment.* Washington, D.C.: The Urban Institute Press.
Benson, Charles, and Gareth Hoachlander
  1981   *Descriptive Study of the Distribution of Federal, State, and Local Funds for Vocational Education.* Final report of the Project on National Vocational Education Resources. School of Education, University of California, Berkeley.
Birch, David
  1981   Who creates jobs? *The Public Interest* (Fall):3-14.
Borus, Michael E.
  1983   A Descriptive Analysis of Employed and Unemployed Youth. Paper prepared for the Committee on Vocational Education and Economic Development in Depressed Areas, National Research Council, Washington, D.C.

84

Bushnell, David S.
  1980   The Role of Vocational Education in Economic Development. State of the
          Practice Report. Prepared under contract number 300-79-0762 with the U.S.
          Department of Education.
Center for Public Resources
  1982   *Basic Skills in the U.S. Work Force: The Contrasting Perceptions of Business,
          Labor, and Public Education.* New York: Center for Public Resources.
College Entrance Examination Board
  1977   *On Further Examination. Report of the Advisory Panel on the Scholastic Aptitude
          Test Score Decline.* Princeton, N.J.: College Board.
Commission on Higher Education and the Economy of New England
  1982   *A Threat to Excellence.* Wenham, Mass.: New England Board of Higher Educa-
          tion.
Committee for Economic Development
  1982   *Public-Private Partnership: An Opportunity for Urban Communities.* New York:
          Committee for Economic Development.
Congressional Budget Office
  1982   *Improving Youth Employment Prospects: Issues and Options.* Washington, D.C.:
          Congressional Budget Office.
Corman, Louise
  1980   *Basic Skills Proficiencies of Secondary Vocational Education Students.* National
          Institute of Education, Vocational Education Study Publication Number 4. Wash-
          ington, D.C.: U.S. Department of Education.
Design for Academic Progress for the 80's Task Force #5
  No   *The Information Economy: Exploiting an Infinite Resource.* New York.
  date
Diaz, William A., Joseph Ball, and Carl Wolfhagen
  1982   *Linking School and Work for Disadvantaged Youths. The YIEPP Demonstration:
          Final Implementation Report.* New York: Manpower Demonstration Research
          Corporation.
Ellwood, David T., and David A. Wise
  1983   *Youth Employment in the Seventies: The Changing Circumstances of Young
          Adults.* Working Paper No. 1055. Cambridge, Mass.: National Bureau of Eco-
          nomic Research, Inc.
Elsman, Max, and the National Institute for Work and Learning
  1981   *Industry-Education-Labor Collaboration: An Action Guide for Collaborative
          Councils.* Available from the Superintendent of Documents (No. 731-147), U.S.
          Government Printing Office. Washington, D.C.: National Institute for Work and
          Learning.
Evans, Rupert N.
  1981   Vocational education and reindustrialization. Pp. 227-251 in Katy B. Green-
          wood, ed., *Contemporary Challenges for Vocational Education.* Arlington, Va.:
          American Vocational Association.
Farkas, George, D. Alton Smith, Ernst W. Stromsdorfer, Gail Trask, and Robert Jerrett
  1982   *Impacts from the Youth Incentive Entitlement Pilot Projects: Participation, Work,
          and Schooling over the Full Program Period.* New York: Manpower Demonstra-
          tion Research Corporation.
Fonte, Richard, and Vernon Magnesen
  1983   Triton College and General Motors: the partnership model. *American Education*
          19(1):22-24.

Fosler, R. Scott, and Renee A. Berger, eds.
  1982   *Public-Private Partnership in American Cities: Seven Case Studies*. Lexington,
          Mass.: D.C. Heath.
Gadway, Charles J., and H. A. Wilson
  1976   *Functional Illiteracy: A Brief Summary and Highlights of an Assessment of
          17-Year-Old Students in 1974 and 1975*. Washington, D.C.: National Assess-
          ment of Education Progress.
Gardner, John A., Paul Campbell, and Patricia Seitz
  1982   *Influences of High School Curriculum on Determinants of Labor Market Ex-
          periences*. Columbus, Ohio: National Center for Research in Vocational Educa-
          tion.
Ginzberg, Eli
  1982   The mechanization of work. *Scientific American* 247(3):67-75.
Glover, Robert W.
  1982   American apprenticeship and disadvantaged youth. Pp. 165-201 in Robert E.
          Taylor, Howard Rosen, and Frank C. Pratzner, eds., *Job Training for Youth: The
          Contributions of the United States Employability Development System*. Colum-
          bus, Ohio: National Center for Research in Vocational Education.
Gold, Gerald G., Bryna Shore Fraser, Max Elsman, and John Raukin
  1981   *Industry-Education-Labor Collaboration: A Directory of Collaborative Coun-
          cils*. Available from the Superintendent of Documents (No. 729-091), U.S.
          Government Printing Office. Washington, D.C.: National Institute for Work and
          Learning.
Grasso, John T., and John R. Shea
  1979a Effects of vocational education programs: research findings and issues. Pp.
          101-192 in *The Planning Papers for the Vocational Education Study*. Washing-
          ton, D.C.: National Institute of Education.
  1979b *Vocational Education and Training: Impact on Youth*. Berkeley, Calif.: Carnegie
          Council on Policy Studies in Higher Education.
Grubb, W. Norton
  1979   The phoenix of vocational education: implications for evaluation. Pp. 195-215 in
          The Planning Papers for the Vocational Education Study. Washington, D.C.:
          National Institute of Education.
Gunn, Thomas G.
  1982   The mechanization of design and manufacturing. *Scientific American* 247(3):115-
          130.
Hanson, Royce, ed.
  1983   *Rethinking Urban Policy: Urban Development in an Advanced Economy*. Com-
          mittee on National Urban Policy, National Research Council. Washington, D.C.:
          National Academy Press.
Levin, Henry M., and Russell W. Rumberger
  1983   High-tech requires few brains. *Washington Post*, January 30.
Levine, Marsha, and Denis P. Doyle
  1982   Private meets public: an examination of contemporary education. Pp. 272-329 in
          Jack A. Meyer, ed., *Meeting Human Needs: Toward a New Public Philosophy*.
          Washington, D.C.: American Enterprise Institute for Public Policy Research.
Lewis, Morgan V., and Donna M. Mertens
  1981   The effects of job training. Pp. 149-165 in Katy B. Greenwood, ed., *Contempo-
          rary Challenges for Vocational Education*. Arlington, Va.: American Vocational
          Association.

Lusterman, S.
1977   *Education in Industry.* New York: The Conference Board.

Mallar, Charles, Stuart Kerachsky, Craig Thornton, David Long, Thomas Good, and Patricia Lapoczynski
1978   *Evaluation of the Economic Impact of the Job Corps Program: First Follow-up Report.* Princeton, N.J.: Mathematica Policy Research.

Mallar, Charles, Stuart Kerachsky, Craig Thornton, Michael Donihue, Carol Jones, David Long, Emmanuel Noggoh, and Jennifer Schore
1980   *Evaluation of the Economic Impact of the Job Corps Program: Second Follow-up Report.* Princeton, N.J.: Mathematica Policy Research.

Martin, Wayne
1981   Student Skills in the Seventies, National Assessment Progress Report. *Compact,* Spring: C1-C4. Reprint 438, Denver, Colo.: Education Commission of the States.

McKinney, Floyd L., Stephen J. Franchak, Ida Halasz-Salster, Irene Morrison, and Douglas McElwain
1981   *Factors Relating to the Job Placement of Former Secondary Vocational Education Students.* Columbus, Ohio: National Center for Research in Vocational Education.

Mertens, D. M., D. McElwain, G. Garcia, and M. Whitmore
1980   *The Effects of Participating in Vocational Education: Summary of Studies Reported Since 1968.* Columbus, Ohio: National Center for Research in Vocational Education.

Meyer, Robert H.
1981a   *An Economic Analysis of High School Vocational Education, I. Vocational Education: How Should It Be Measured?* Washington, D.C.: The Urban Institute.
1981b   *An Economic Analysis of High School Vocational Education, II. The Determinants of Participants in Vocational Education: The Role of Schools and Personal Characteristics.* Washington, D.C.: The Urban Institute.
1981c   *An Economic Analysis of High School Vocational Education, III. The Effect of Vocational Education on Post Secondary School Choices.* Washington, D.C.: The Urban Institute.
1981d   *An Economic Analysis of High School Vocational Education, IV. The Labor Market Effects of Vocational Education.* Washington, D.C.: The Urban Institute.

Meyer, Robert H., and David A. Wise
1982a   High school preparation and early labor force experience. In Richard B. Freeman and David A. Wise, eds., *The Youth Labor Market Problem: Its Nature, Causes, and Consequences.* Chicago: University of Chicago Press.
1982b   *The Transition from School to Work: The Experiences of Blacks and Whites.* Working Paper No. 1007. Cambridge, Mass.: National Bureau of Economic Research.

National Academy of Sciences and National Academy of Engineering
1982   *Science and Mathematics in the Schools: Report of a Convocation.* Washington, D.C.: National Academy Press.

National Association of State Directors of Vocational Education
1981   *The Role and Responsibility of Vocational Education in Economic Development and Productivity.* Arlington, Va.: National Association of State Directors of Vocational Education.

National Center for Education Statistics
  1981   *The Condition of Vocational Education*. Prepared by Mary A. Golladay and Rolf
          M. Wulfsberg. Washington, D.C.: U.S. Department of Education.
National Commission for Employment Policy
  1981   *The Federal Role in Vocation Education*. Washington, D.C.: National Commis-
          sion for Employment Policy.
  1982   *8th Annual Report: The Work Revolution*. Report No. 15. Washington, D.C.:
          National Commission for Employment Policy.
National Commission on Excellence in Education
  1983   *A Nation at Risk: The Imperative for Educational Reform*. Washington, D.C.:
          National Commission on Excellence in Education.
National Institute of Education
  1980   *The Vocational Education Study: The Interim Report*. Publication No. 3. Wash-
          ington, D.C.: National Institute of Education.
  1981   *The Vocational Education Study: The Final Report*. Publication No. 8. Washing-
          ton, D.C.: National Institute of Education.
National Occupational Information Coordinating Committee
  1982   *Vocational Preparation and Occupations*, 3d ed. *Vol. 1.: Education and Occupa-
          tional Code Crosswalk*. Washington, D.C.: U.S. Department of Education.
New York City Public Schools
  No   *Training Opportunities Program 1981-82. Final Evaluation Report, Board of
  date   Education Project I.D. #0427*. New York: Office of Educational Evaluation,
          New York City Public Schools.
Nuñez, Ann R., and Jill Frymier Russell
  1981   *Manufacturers' Views of Vocational Education*. Columbus, Ohio: National Cen-
          ter for Research in Vocational Education.
Office of Technology Assessment
  1983   *Automation and the Workplace: Selected Labor, Education and Training Issues*.
          Washington, D.C.: Office of Technology Assessment.
Paul, Krishan K., and Ellen A. Carlos
  1981   *Vocational Educators' Handbook for Economic Development*. Arlington, Va.:
          American Vocational Association.
Robison, David
  1978   *Training and Jobs Programs in Action: Case Studies in Private-Sector Initiatives
          for the Hard-to-Employ*. New York: Committee for Economic Development;
          Scarsdale, N.Y.: Work in America Institute, Inc.
Rosenfeld, Stuart
  1981   *A Portrait of Rural America: Conditions Affecting Vocational Education Policy*.
          Vocational Education Study Publication No. 6. Washington, D.C.: National
          Institute of Education.
Schilit, Henrietta, and Richard Lacey
  1982   *The Private Sector Youth Connection. Volume 1: School to Work: A Planning
          Manual for Educators and Business People*. New York: Vocational Foundation,
          Inc.
SER/Jobs for Progress
  No   *The Federal Role in Vocational Education*. Dallas: SER/Jobs for Progress.
  date
Stanback, Thomas M. Jr., Peter J. Bearse, Thierry J. Noyelle, and Robert A. Karasek
  1981   *Services: The New Economy*. Totowa, N.J.: Allanheld, Osmun & Co.

Stromsdorfer, Ernst W.
   1979   The effectiveness of youth programs: an analysis of the historical antecedents of current youth initiatives. Pp. 88-111 in Bernard E. Anderson and Isabel V. Sawhill, eds., *Youth Employment and Public Policy*. Englewood Cliffs, N.J.: Prentice-Hall.

Sullivan, Sean
   1983   Private Initiatives to Improve Youth Employment. Paper prepared for the Committee on Vocational Education and Economic Development in Depressed Areas, National Research Council, Washington, D.C.

Taggart, Robert
   1981   *A Fisherman's Guide: An Assessment of Training and Remediation Strategies*. Kalamazoo, Mich.: W. E. Upjohn Institute for Employment Research.

Task Force on Education for Economic Growth
   1983   *Action for Excellence: A Comprehensive Plan to Improve Our Nation's Schools*. Denver: Education Commission of the States.

Twentieth Century Fund
   1983   Report of the Twentieth Century Fund Task Force on Federal Elementary and Secondary Education Policy. Prepublication copy. New York: Twentieth Century Fund, Inc.

U.S. Department of Education
   1981   *Vocational Education*. Report by the Secretary of Education to the Congress. Washington, D.C.: U.S. Department of Education.

U.S. Department of Health, Education, and Welfare, Office of Planning, Budgeting, and Evaluation
   1978   *National Study of Vocational Education Systems and Facilities*. Washington, D.C.: U.S. Department of Health, Education, and Welfare.

Vedder, Richard K.
   1982   *Robotics and the Economy*. Staff study for the Subcommittee on Monetary and Fiscal Policy of the Joint Economic Committee, Congress of the United States, March 26, 1982. Washington, D.C.: U.S. Government Printing Office.

Worthington, Robert M.
   1981   Re-Thinking Education and Work in the United States for the 1980's. Paper presented to the UNESCO International Conference in Education, Geneva, Switzerland, November 10-19.
   1982   Youth employability in the context of the 1980's. In Robert E. Taylor, Howard Rosen, and Frank C. Pratzner, eds., *Job Training for Youth*. Columbus, Ohio: National Center for Research in Vocational Education.

APPENDIX *A* Selected Tables on
Youth Employment
and Unemployment

The following tables are drawn from "A Descriptive Analysis of Employed and Unemployed Youth," written for the committee by Michael E. Borus. The paper will appear in modified form in a book on youth employment problems to be published by W. E. Upjohn Institute for Employment Research. These tables were created from data in the National Longitudinal Surveys of Youth Labor Market Experience.

The National Longitudinal Surveys of Youth Labor Market Experience are conducted annually with over 12,000 young people. When weighted, as in the following tables, they represent the national population born in the years 1957 through 1964 (for further details on the NLS, see the *National Longitudinal Surveys Handbook* published by the Center for Human Resource Research, Ohio State University, 1982). Special analyses were made for this report using the spring 1981 survey wave. These data are used to describe the characteristics of employed and unemployed young people as of that time. Most of the analyses are limited to those who were ages 16-21 at the time of that interview. Since the interviews were conducted in spring 1981, some born in 1965 had their 16th birthday prior to the interview and are excluded from the NLS. As a result, the data presented here underrepresent 16-year-olds, including only those whose birthdays fell after the spring. The approximately 800,000 youngest 16-year-olds in the population are not represented in the sample. This biases slightly the employment-to-population ratios (upward) and the unemployment rates (downward).

91

Some questions on discrimination and other perceived barriers to employment were asked of all young people in 1979 and were not repeated. For these variables, the data presented include all those ages 16-22 as of spring 1979. It is unlikely that there have been substantial changes in these perceptions between 1979 and the present.

TABLE A-1 Percentage Distribution of Young People Ages 16-21, by Sex, Employment Status, and Age, Spring 1981

	16	17	18	19	20	21	Total
Females							
Employed	38	43	52	60	62	61	53
	(581)	(893)	(1,034)	(1,225)	(1,244)	(1,242)	(6,218)
Unemployed	16	17	15	11	7	10	12
	(245)	(353)	(303)	(214)	(140)	(210)	(1,466)
Out of labor	46	40	33	30	31	29	34
force	(710)	(830)	(650)	(610)	(633)	(597)	(4,030)
Unemployment rate	30	28	23	15	10	15	19
Males							
Employed	38	50	57	64	64	84	58
	(620)	(1,071)	(1,096)	(1,232)	(1,244)	(1,474)	(6,736)
Unemployed	18	22	17	15	15	10	16
	(296)	(463)	(323)	(285)	(291)	(192)	(1,849)
Out of labor	44	29	26	21	21	16	26
force	(729)	(612)	(492)	(413)	(402)	(325)	(2,973)
Unemployment rate	32	30	23	19	19	12	22
Total							
Employed	38	47	55	62	63	67	56
	(1,201)	(1,965)	(2,129)	(2,457)	(2,487)	(2,715)	(12,954)
Unemployed	18	19	16	13	11	10	14
	(541)	(816)	(625)	(500)	(431)	(402)	(3,315)
Out of labor	45	34	29	26	26	23	30
force	(1,439)	(1,442)	(1,142)	(1,023)	(1,035)	(922)	(7,002)
Unemployment rate	31	29	23	17	15	13	20

NOTE: Those age 16 born in 1965 (i.e., those having their birthday between January 1, 1981, and the interview date) are not included. This reduces the number of 16-year-olds by approximately 21 percent. Numbers in parentheses represent thousands.

TABLE A-2   Percentage Distribution of Young People Ages 16-21, by Sex, Employment Status, and Race, Spring 1981

	Black	Hispanic	White	Total
Females				
Employed	35	47	57	53
	(582)	(341)	(5,296)	(6,218)
Unemployed	22	12	11	12
	(364)	(90)	(1,011)	(1,466)
Out of labor	43	41	32	34
force	(715)	(298)	(3,018)	(4,030)
Unemployment				
rate	38	21	16	19
Males				
Employed	45	57	61	58
	(714)	(422)	(5,601)	(6,736)
Unemployed	24	20	14	16
	(383)	(151)	(1,315)	(1,849)
Out of labor	31	23	25	26
force	(495)	(168)	(2,310)	(2,973)
Unemployment				
rate	35	26	23	22
Total				
Employed	40	52	59	56
	(1,296)	(762)	(10,896)	(12,954)
Unemployed	23	16	12	14
	(747)	(242)	(2,326)	(3,315)
Out of labor	37	32	29	30
Force	(1,209)	(466)	(5,328)	(7,002)
Unemployment				
rate	37	24	18	20

NOTE: Those age 16 born in 1965 (i.e., those having their birthday between January 1, 1981, and the interview date) are not included. This reduces the number of 16-year-olds by approximately 21 percent. Numbers in parentheses represent thousands.

TABLE A-3   Percentage Distribution of Young People Ages 16-21, by Sex, Employment Status, and Enrollment Status, Spring 1981

	Enrollment Status as of 1981 Interview				
	High-School Dropout	Enrolled in High School	Enrolled in College	High School Graduate, Not Enrolled	Total
Females					
Employed	33	43	52	72	53
	(522)	(1,615)	(1,295)	(2,781)	(6,218)
Unemployed	20	15	6	12	12
	(309)	(555)	(153)	(448)	(1,466)
Out of labor	47	42	42	17	34
force	(730)	(1,583)	(1,064)	(646)	(4,030)
Unemployment					
rate	37	26	11	14	19
Males					
Employed	60	45	52	79	58
	(1,082)	(1,871)	(1,232)	(2,551)	(6,736)
Unemployed	25	18	6	15	16
	(447)	(767)	(150)	(479)	(1,849)
Out of labor	15	36	41	6	26
force	(269)	(1,518)	(972)	(212)	(2,973)
Unemployment					
rate	29	29	11	16	22
Total					
Employed	48	44	52	75	56
	(1,603)	(3,486)	(2,527)	(5,332)	(12,954)
Unemployed	22	17	6	13	14
	(756)	(1,322)	(303)	(928)	(3,315)
Out of labor	30	39	42	12	30
force	(1,000)	(3,101)	(2,037)	(859)	(7,002)
Unemployment					
rate	32	27	11	15	20

NOTE: Those age 16 born in 1965 (i.e., those having their birthday between January 1, 1981, and the interview date) are not included. This reduces the number of 16-year-olds by approximately 21 percent. Numbers in parentheses represent thousands. School enrollment status was not available for 17,500 young people.

TABLE A-4 Percentage Distribution of Young People Ages 16-21, by Sex, Employment Status, and Educational Attainment, Spring 1981

	Highest Grade Completed as of 1981 Interview						
	Less Than 8th Grade	Some High School	12th Grade	1-3 Years College	4 Years College	Graduate School	Total
Females							
Employed	20	42	65	62	96	0	53
	(71)	(2,065)	(2,702)	(1,356)	(18)	(0)	(6,218)
Unemployed	22	16	12	5	4	0	12
	(74)	(790)	(488)	(113)	(1)	(0)	(1,466)
Out of labor	58	42	24	33	0	0	34
force	(199)	(2,114)	(984)	(727)	(0)	(0)	(4,030)
Unemployment							
rate	51	28	15	8	5	0	19
Males							
Employed	49	50	72	58	92	100	58
	(224)	(2,729)	(2,797)	(972)	(13)	(1)	(6,736)
Unemployed	26	20	13	6	0	0	16
	(119)	(1,095)	(521)	(108)	(0)	(0)	(1,849)
Out of labor	25	30	15	36	8	0	26
force	(116)	(1,671)	(573)	(611)	(1)	(0)	(2,973)
Unemployment							
rate	35	29	16	10	0	0	22
Total							
Employed	37	46	68	60	94	100	56
	(294)	(4,795)	(5,499)	(2,328)	(31)	(1)	(12,954)
Unemployed	24	18	12	6	2	0	14
	(194)	(1,885)	(1,008)	(222)	(1)	(0)	(3,314)
Out of labor	39	36	19	34	3	0	30
force	(315)	(3,785)	(1,557)	(1,338)	(1)	(0)	(7,002)
Unemployment							
rate	40	28	15	9	3	0	20

NOTE: Those age 16 born in 1965 (i.e., those having their birthday between January 1, 1981, and the interview date) are not included. This reduces the number of 16-year-olds by approximately 21 percent. Numbers in parentheses represent thousands. Educational attainment was not available for 17,500 young people.

TABLE A-5   Percentage Distribution of Young People Ages 16-21, by Sex, Employment Status, and Marital Status, Spring 1981

| | Marital Status | | | | |
	Never Married	Married, Spouse Present	Other	Not Available	Total
Females					
Employed	54	48	53	43	53
	(5,104)	(902)	(151)	(61)	(6,218)
Unemployed	12	12	19	19	12
	(1,165)	(218)	(55)	(27)	(1,466)
Out of labor	33	41	28	38	34
force	(3,126)	(769)	(81)	(53)	(4,030)
Unemployment					
rate	19	19	27	31	19
Males					
Employed	56	85	87	65	58
	(5,868)	(662)	(87)	(118)	(6,736)
Unemployed	16	12	10	18	16
	(1,713)	(94)	(10)	(32)	(1,849)
Out of labor	28	3	3	17	26
force	(2,912)	(25)	(3)	(32)	(2,973)
Unemployment					
rate	23	12	10	21	22
Total					
Employed	55	59	62	55	56
	(10,972)	(1,564)	(238)	(179)	(12,949)
Unemployed	14	12	17	18	14
	(2,878)	(312)	(64)	(60)	(3,314)
Out of labor	30	30	22	26	30
force	(6,039)	(794)	(94)	(85)	(7,002)
Unemployment					
rate	29	17	21	25	20

NOTE: Those age 16 born in 1965 (i.e., those having their birthday between January 1, 1981, and the interview date) are not included. This reduces the number of 16-year-olds by approximately 21 percent. Numbers in parentheses represent thousands. Information on marital status was not available for 323,700 young people.

TABLE A-6 Percentage Distribution of Young People Ages 16-21, by Sex, Employment Status, and Presence of Respondent's Children in the Household, Spring 1981

	Children in Household	Children Not in Household	Total
Females			
Employed	33	57	53
	(564)	(5,654)	(6,218)
Unemployed	15	12	12
	(258)	(1,202)	(1,466)
Out of labor	52	31	34
force	(902)	(3,126)	(4,030)
Unemployment			
rate	31	18	19
Males			
Employed	76	58	58
	(342)	(6,394)	(6,736)
Unemployed	17	16	16
	(76)	(1,773)	(1,849)
Out of labor	8	26	26
force	(34)	(2,939)	(2,973)
Unemployment			
rate	18	22	22
Total			
Employed	42	57	56
	(905)	(12,049)	(12,949)
Unemployed	15	14	14
	(334)	(2,976)	(3,314)
Out of labor	43	29	30
force	(936)	(6,065)	(7,002)
Unemployment			
rate	27	20	20

NOTE: Those age 16 born in 1965 (i.e., those having their birthday between January 1, 1981, and the interview date) are not included. This reduces the number of 16-year-olds by approximately 21 percent. Numbers in parentheses represent thousands. Information on children in the household was not available for 6,900 young people.

TABLE A-7   Percentage Distribution of Young People Ages 16-21, by Sex, Employment Status, and Living Arrangements at Time of 1981 Interview

	Living with Parents	Away From Household in College or Military	Living in Own Household	Total
Females				
Employed	54	39	54	53
	(4,007)	(398)	(1,813)	(6,218)
Unemployed	14	3	11	12
	(1,071)	(34)	(360)	(1,466)
Out of labor	31	57	35	34
force	(2,292)	(580)	(1,158)	(4,030)
Unemployment				
rate	21	8	17	19
Males				
Employed	57	34	77	58
	(4,888)	(365)	(1,484)	(6,736)
Unemployed	18	7	12	16
	(1,556)	(70)	(222)	(1,849)
Out of labor	25	59	12	26
force	(2,210)	(630)	(223)	(2,973)
Unemployment				
rate	24	16	13	22
Total				
Employed	56	37	63	56
	(8,891)	(763)	(3,296)	(12,949)
Unemployed	16	5	11	14
	(2,628)	(104)	(583)	(3,314)
Out of labor	28	58	26	30
force	(4,412)	(1,210)	(1,381)	(7,002)
Unemployment				
rate	23	12	15	20

NOTE: Those age 16 born in 1965 (i.e., those having their birthday between January 1, 1981, and the interview date) are not included. This reduces the number of 16-year-olds by approximately 21 percent. Numbers in parentheses represent thousands.

TABLE A-8 Percentage Distribution of Young People Ages 16-21, by Sex, Employment Status, and Region of Residence, Spring 1981

	Northeast	North Central	South	West	Total
Females					
Employed	56	56	46	59	53
	(1,271)	(1,966)	(1,871)	(1,109)	(6,218)
Unemployed	14	11	13	13	12
	(312)	(391)	(515)	(248)	(1,466)
Out of labor	31	33	41	28	34
force	(709)	(1,140)	(1,648)	(531)	(4,030)
Unemployment					
rate	20	17	22	18	19
Males					
Employed	62	56	55	65	58
	(1,453)	(2,022)	(2,025)	(1,234)	(6,736)
Unemployed	12	21	14	14	16
	(287)	(751)	(535)	(276)	(1,849)
Out of labor	26	23	30	20	26
force	(618)	(839)	(1,123)	(386)	(2,973)
Unemployment					
rate	16	27	21	18	22
Total					
Employed	59	56	50	62	56
	(2,724)	(3,988)	(3,896)	(2,343)	(12,949)
Unemployed	13	16	14	14	14
	(599)	(1,142)	(1,050)	(523)	(3,314)
Out of labor	28	28	36	24	30
force	(1,327)	(1,980)	(2,770)	(917)	(7,002)
Unemployment					
rate	18	22	21	18	20

NOTE: Those age 16 born in 1965 (i.e., those having their birthday between January 1, 1981, and the interview date) are not included. This reduces the number of 16-year-olds by approximately 21 percent. Numbers in parentheses represent thousands. Information on region of residence was not available for 12,600 young people.

TABLE A-9 Percentage Distribution of Young People Ages 16-21, by Sex, Employment Status, and Residence in Rural or Urban Area, Spring 1981

	Rural	Urban	Total
Females			
Employed	48	54	53
	(1,252)	(4,956)	(6,218)
Unemployed	11	13	12
	(281)	(1,185)	(1,466)
Out of labor	41	32	34
force	(1,072)	(2,956)	(4,030)
Unemployment			
rate	18	19	19
Males			
Employed	54	60	58
	(1,411)	(5,320)	(6,736)
Unemployed	15	16	16
	(389)	(1,460)	(1,849)
Out of labor	31	24	26
force	(798)	(2,155)	(2,973)
Unemployment			
rate	22	22	22
Total			
Employed	51	57	56
	(2,663)	(10,271)	(12,949)
Unemployed	13	15	14
	(670)	(2,644)	(3,314)
Out of labor	36	28	30
force	(1,870)	(5,122)	(7,002)
Unemployment			
rate	20	20	20

NOTE: Those age 16 born in 1965 (i.e., those having their birthday between January 1, 1981, and the interview date) are not included. This reduces the number of 16-year-olds by approximately 21 percent. Numbers in parentheses represent thousands. Information on area of residence was not available for 25,100 young people.

TABLE A-10 Percentage Distribution of Young People Ages 16-21, by Sex, Employment Status, and Residence in the Central City of a Standard Metropolitan Statistical Area (SMSA), Spring 1981

	Not in SMSA	In SMSA, Not in Central City	In Central City of SMSA	In SMSA, Residence in Central City Unknown	Total
Females					
Employed	48	57	47	56	53
	(1,429)	(2,263)	(1,005)	(1,436)	(6,218)
Unemployed	12	12	15	13	12
	(364)	(466)	(310)	(327)	(1,466)
Out of labor	40	31	38	32	34
force	(1,168)	(1,212)	(804)	(825)	(4,030)
Unemployment					
rate	20	17	24	19	19
Males					
Employed	56	61	56	59	58
	(1,756)	(2,301)	(1,182)	(1,455)	(6,736)
Unemployed	16	15	17	18	16
	(490)	(550)	(365)	(444)	(1,849)
Out of labor	28	24	27	23	26
force	(894)	(909)	(574)	(576)	(2,973)
Unemployment					
rate	22	19	24	23	22
Total					
Employed	52	59	52	57	56
	(3,186)	(4,564)	(2,187)	(2,891)	(12,949)
Unemployed	14	13	16	15	14
	(853)	(1,016)	(675)	(770)	(3,314)
Out of labor	34	27	32	28	30
force	(2,062)	(2,121)	(1,378)	(1,402)	(7,002)
Unemployment					
rate	21	18	24	21	20

NOTE: Those age 16 born in 1965 (i.e., those having their birthday between January 1, 1981, and the interview date) are not included. This reduces the number of 16-year-olds by approximately 21 percent. Numbers in parentheses represent thousands. Information on residence location in an SMSA was not available for 165,800 young people.

TABLE A-11 Percentage Distribution of Young People Ages 16-21, by Sex, Employment Status, and Local Unemployment Rate in County of Residence, Spring 1981

	Unemployment Rate					
	3.0-5.9%	6.0-8.9%	9.0-11.9%	12.0-14.9%	Unknown	Total
Females						
Employed	57	53	42	51	40	53
	(2,325)	(2,971)	(455)	(384)	(82)	(6,218)
Unemployed	12	12	13	18	22	12
	(490)	(656)	(142)	(133)	(45)	(1,466)
Out of labor	31	35	45	32	37	34
force	(1,287)	(1,939)	(490)	(240)	(74)	(4,030)
Unemployment						
rate	17	18	24	26	35	19
Males						
Employed	61	57	51	62	64	58
	(2,397)	(3,136)	(502)	(529)	(172)	(6,736)
Unemployed	14	16	22	21	22	16
	(537)	(857)	(219)	(177)	(58)	(1,849)
Out of labor	26	28	27	17	14	26
force	(1,019)	(1,511)	(263)	(141)	(38)	(2,973)
Unemployment						
rate	18	21	30	25	25	22
Total						
Employed	59	55	46	57	54	56
	(4,723)	(6,107)	(958)	(913)	(253)	(12,949)
Unemployed	13	14	17	19	22	14
	(1,026)	(1,514)	(361)	(310)	(103)	(3,314)
Out of labor	29	31	36	24	24	30
force	(2,306)	(3,450)	(753)	(381)	(112)	(7,002)
Unemployment						
rate	18	20	27	25	29	20

NOTE: Those age 16 born in 1965 (i.e., those having their birthday between January 1, 1981, and the interview date) are not included. This reduces the number of 16-year-olds by approximately 21 percent. Numbers in parentheses represent thousands.

TABLE A-12 Percentage Distribution of Unemployed Young People Ages 16-21, by Sex and Reasons for Looking for Work, Spring 1981

Reason Looking for Work	Females	Males	Total
Need money	50	48	49
	(737)	(879)	(1,616)
Lost job	8	12	11
	(125)	(228)	(353)
Quit job	10	8	9
	(151)	(151)	(302)
Family expenses	5	3	4
	(71)	(50)	(121)
Support self	3	3	3
	(40)	(56)	(96)
Left school	2	4	3
	(32)	(69)	(100)
Enjoy working	5	2	3
	(7)	(29)	(96)
Other	11	11	11
	(168)	(206)	(374)
No reason given	5	10	8
	(76)	(180)	(256)
Total	100	100	100
	(1,466)	(1,849)	(3,315)

NOTE: Persons 16 years of age born in 1965 (i.e., those having their birthday between January 1, 1981, and the interview date) are not included. This reduces the number of 16-year-olds by approximately 21 percent. Numbers in parentheses represent thousands.

TABLE A-13   Percentage Distribution of Unemployed Young People Ages 16-21, by Sex and Method of Job Search, Spring 1981

Method of Job Search	Females	Males	Total
Checked directly with employer	58	58	58
Looked in newspaper	38	26	31
Placed or answered ads	16	8	11
Checked with state employment agency	15	17	16
Used school employment service	6	5	6
Checked with private employment agency	4	3	4
Checked with friends or relatives	14	18	16
Other method	10	9	10

NOTE: Persons 16 years of age born in 1965 (i.e., those having their birthday between January 1, 1981, and the interview date) are not included. This reduces the number of 16-year-olds by approximately 21 percent.

TABLE A-14 Percentage Distribution of Unemployed Young People Ages 16-21, by Sex and Occupation Sought, Spring 1981

Occupation Sought	Females	Males	Total
Professional, technical, and kindred	4	3	3
	(52)	(55)	(107)
Managers and administrators	0	1	1
	(2)	(20)	(22)
Sales workers	12	4	8
	(74)	(77)	(251)
Clerical and kindred	28	5	15
	(415)	(85)	(500)
Craftsmen and kindred	1	12	7
	(20)	(215)	(235)
Operatives, except transport	2	6	5
	(34)	(117)	(151)
Transport equipment operatives	0	3	2
	(5)	(51)	(56)
Laborers, except farm	2	14	9
	(30)	(255)	(285)
Farmers and farm managers	0	0	0
	(0)	(0)	(0)
Farm laborers and foremen	0	1	1
	(1)	(18)	(19)
Service workers, except private	20	12	16
	(291)	(225)	(516)
Private household workers	3	0	1
	(47)	(0)	(47)
Any kind of job	27	40	34
	(396)	(731)	(1,127)
Total	100	100	100
	(1,466)	(1,849)	(3,315)

NOTE: Persons 16 years of age born in 1965 (i.e., those having their birthday between January 1, 1981, and the interview date) are not included. This reduces the number of 16-year-olds by approximately 21 percent. Numbers in parentheses represent thousands.

TABLE A-15 Percentage Distribution of Unemployed Young People Ages 16-21, by Sex and Minimum Hourly Wage Necessary to Induce them to Accept a Job for Which They Were Looking, Spring 1981

Reservation Wage	Females	Males	Total
Less than $2.50	2	1	2
	(32)	(24)	(57)
$2.50-$2.99	1	2	1
	(17)	(28)	(44)
$3.00-$3.24	11	8	9
	(160)	(148)	(309)
$3.25-$3.34	8	7	7
	(118)	(123)	(241)
$3.35 (federal minimum wage)	38	33	36
	(561)	(616)	(1,176)
$3.36-$3.49	4	2	3
	(58)	(40)	(98)
$3.50-$3.99	14	12	12
	(200)	(212)	(412)
$4.00-$4.49	8	13	11
	(110)	(241)	(350)
$4.50-$4.99	2	3	2
	(27)	(58)	(84)
$5.00-$5.49	3	6	5
	(50)	(117)	(166)
$5.50 or more	3	7	5
	(42)	(127)	(169)
Data not available	6	6	6
	(91)	(116)	(207)
Total	100	100	100
	(1,466)	(1,849)	(3,315)

NOTE: Persons 16 years of age born in 1965 (i.e., those having their birthday between January 1, 1981, and the interview date) are not included. This reduces the number of 16-year-olds by approximately 21 percent. Numbers in parentheses represent thousands.

TABLE A-16   Percentage Distribution of Employed Young People
Ages 16-21, by Sex and Occupation, Spring 1981

Occupation	Females	Males	Total
Professional, technical,	4	4	4
and kindred	(257)	(299)	(556)
Managers and	2	3	2
administrators	(140)	(184)	(324)
Sales workers	10	7	8
	(598)	(488)	(1,086)
Clerical and kindred	37	9	23
	(2,306)	(632)	(2,938)
Craftsmen and kindred	2	14	8
	(110)	(971)	(1,081)
Operatives, except	6	13	10
transport	(372)	(885)	(1,257)
Transport equipment	0	5	3
operatives	(21)	(314)	(336)
Laborers, except farm	2	18	10
	(100)	(1,223)	(1,323)
Farmers and farm	0	3	2
laborers	(34)	(229)	(263)
Service workers except	30	22	26
private household	(1,883)	(1,493)	(3,376)
Private household	6	0	3
workers	(386)	(13)	(399)
Total	100	100	100
	(6,218)	(6,736)	(12,954)

NOTE: Persons 16 years of age born in 1965 (i.e., those having their birthday between
January 1, 1981, and the interview date) are not included. This reduces the number of
16-year-olds by approximately 21 percent. Numbers in parentheses represent thousands.

TABLE A-17 Percentage Distribution of Employed Young People Ages 16-21, by Sex and Industry, Spring 1981

Industry	Females	Males	Total
Agriculture, forestry and fisheries	1 (66)	5 (315)	3 (380)
Mining	0 (9)	2 (101)	1 (110)
Construction	0 (18)	8 (559)	4 (577)
Manufacturing, durable goods	5 (289)	11 (725)	8 (1,014)
Manufacturing, nondurable goods	6 (389)	8 (530)	7 (912)
Transportation, communications, and other public utilities	2 (118)	3 (182)	2 (300)
Wholesale trade	2 (118)	4 (234)	3 (352)
Retail trade	38 (2,368)	34 (2,318)	36 (4,686)
Finance, insurance, and real estate	8 (494)	2 (127)	5 (621)
Business and repair services	2 (130)	8 (513)	5 (644)
Personal services	10 (600)	3 (194)	6 (794)
Entertainment and recreation services	2 (109)	3 (174)	2 (283)
Professional and related services	22 (1,362)	10 (641)	16 (2,004)
Public administration	2 (150)	2 (107)	2 (256)
Total	100 (6,218)	100 (6,736)	100 (12,954)

NOTE: Persons 16 years of age born in 1965 (i.e., those having their birthday between January 1, 1981, and the interview date) are not included. This reduces the number of 16-year-olds by approximately 21 percent. Numbers in parentheses represent thousands.

TABLE A-18 Percentage Distribution of Employed Young People Ages 16-21, by Sex and Hours Worked, Spring 1981

Hours Usually Worked per Week	Females	Males	Total
0-19	31	24	28
	(1,934)	(1,639)	(3,573)
20-34	25	25	25
	(1,553)	(1,689)	(3,242)
35-40	38	34	36
	(2,370)	(2,259)	(4,629)
40 or more	5	16	11
	(328)	(1,095)	(1,423)
Total	100	100	100
	(6,218)	(6,736)	(12,954)

NOTE: Persons 16 years of age born in 1965 (i.e., those having their birthday between January 1, 1981, and the interview date) are not included. This reduces the number of 16-year-olds by approximately 21 percent. Numbers in parentheses represent thousands.

TABLE A-19 Percentage Distribution of Employed Young People Ages 16-21, by Sex and Shifts Worked, Spring 1981

Shifts Usually Worked	Females	Males	Total
Day	50	47	49
	(3,126)	(3,165)	(6,291)
Evening	15	16	16
	(959)	(1,094)	(2,054)
Night	6	8	7
	(352)	(536)	(888)
Split	3	4	3
	(174)	(234)	(408)
Variable hours	25	25	25
	(1,588)	(1,686)	(3,274)
Total	100	100	100
	(6,218)	(6,736)	(12,954)

NOTE: Persons 16 years of age born in 1965 (i.e., those having their birthday between January 1, 1981, and the interview date) are not included. This reduces the number of 16-year-olds by approximately 21 percent. Numbers in parentheses represent thousands.

TABLE A-20   Percentage Distribution of Employed Young People Ages 16-21, by Sex and Hourly Wage, Spring 1981

Hourly Wage	Females	Males	Total
Less than $2.50	11	5	8
	(676)	(335)	(1,011)
$2.50-$2.99	5	5	5
	(334)	(323)	(657)
$3.00-$3.24	6	6	6
	(402)	(410)	(813)
$3.25-$3.34	4	4	4
	(231)	(252)	(483)
$3.35 (federal minimum wage)	13	10	11
	(820)	(662)	(1,482)
$3.36-$3.49	6	4	5
	(368)	(255)	(623)
$3.50-$3.99	17	15	16
	(1,037)	(1,021)	(2,058)
$4.00-$4.49	12	12	12
	(771)	(802)	(1,573)
$5.00-$5.49	6	8	7
	(374)	(510)	(884)
$5.50 or more	22	15	19
	(1,488)	(926)	(2,414)
Data not available	4	4	4
	(274)	(241)	(515)
Total	100	100	100
	(6,218)	(6,736)	(12,954)

NOTE: Persons 16 years of age born in 1965 (i.e., those having their birthday between January 1, 1981, and the interview date) are not included. This reduces the number of 16-year-olds by approximately 21 percent. Numbers in parentheses represent thousands.

TABLE A-21   Percentage Distribution of Employed Young People Ages 16-21, by Sex and General Education Required by Occupation, Spring 1981

General Education Required	Females	Males	Total
Up to 8 years	17	38	28
	(1,074)	(2,526)	(3,600)
9-11 years	59	44	51
	(3,682)	(2,968)	(6,650)
12 years	16	12	14
	(1,021)	(779)	(1,800)
Over 12 years	5	7	6
	(331)	(458)	(790)
Total	100	100	100
	(6,218)	(6,736)	(12,954)

NOTE: Persons 16 years of age born in 1965 (i.e., those having their birthday between January 1, 1981, and the interview date) are not included. This reduces the number of 16-year-olds by approximately 21 percent. Numbers in parentheses represent thousands.

TABLE A-22   Percentage Distribution of Employed Young People Ages 16-21, by Sex and Specific Vocational Preparation Required by Occupation, Spring 1981

Vocational Preparation Required	Females	Males	Total
Short demonstration	49	44	46
	(3,037)	(2,974)	(6,012)
Up to and including 30 days	21	22	22
	(1,327)	(1,465)	(2,792)
31 days, up to and including 3 months	22	16	19
	(1,349)	(1,057)	(2,406)
3 months, up to and including 6 months	4	13	8
	(235)	(848)	(1,084)
6 months to 1 year	2	2	2
	(116)	(170)	(286)
1 to 2 years	1	2	1
	(73)	(112)	(185)
More than 2 years	1	2	1
	(71)	(105)	(175)
Total	100	100	100
	(6,218)	(6,736)	(12,954)

NOTE: Persons 16 years of age born in 1965 (i.e., those having their birthday between January 1, 1981, and the interview date) are not included. This reduces the number of 16-year-olds by approximately 21 percent. Numbers in parentheses represent thousands.

TABLE A-23   Percentage Distribution of Young People Ages 16-22 Indicating That Certain Problems Had Caused Them Difficulty in Getting a Good Job, by Sex and Race, Spring 1979

Problem	Females			Males			Total
	Black	Hispanic	White	Black	Hispanic	White	
Age discrimination	46	44	47	47	47	42	45
Sex discrimination	17	13	13	7	5	4	9
Race or nationality discrimination	22	16	3	21	20	4	7
Lack of transportation	37	37	30	43	35	25	30
Lack of experience	13	16	17	11	12	11	14
Lack of education	7	12	6	6	7	5	6
Problem with English	4	18	2	5	18	2	3

SOURCE: David Shapiro, 1981, "Perceptions of Discrimination and Other Barriers to Employment," p. 482 in Michael E. Borus, ed., *Pathways to the Future*. Columbus: Center for Human Resource Research.

APPENDIX *B* Biographical Sketches of Committee Members and Staff

COLIN C. BLAYDON became dean of the Amos Tuck School of Business Administration at Dartmouth College in fall 1980. From 1975 until 1983 he was vice provost for academic policy and planning and professor of policy sciences and business administration at Duke University. From 1973 to 1975 he was deputy associate director, Office of Management and Budget. He has conducted wide-ranging research in finance, budgeting, and regulatory economics. He holds A.M. and Ph.D. degrees in applied mathematics from Harvard University and a B.A. degree in electrical engineering from the University of Virginia.

WILLIAM A. MORRILL has been president of Mathematica Policy Research in Princeton, New Jersey, since 1977. Before that he held posts in the Energy Policy and Planning Office of the White House; the Office of Planning and Evaluation in the U.S. Department of Health, Education, and Welfare; the Office of Management and Budget; and several defense-related government offices. He has a master's degree in public administration from Syracuse University and a bachelor's degree from Wesleyan University.

CHARLES S. BENSON is professor of the economics of education at the University of California at Berkeley, a position he has held since 1964. His research has focused on resource allocations in education, public-sector cost and revenue projections, and productivity analysis in the public sector, and he has considerable consulting experience in the education programs of foreign countries. He has M.A. and Ph.D. degrees from Columbia University and a B.A. degree from Princeton University, all in economics.

CHARLES E. BRADFORD is director of the organizing department of the International Association of Machinists and Aerospace Workers, where he also served as director of the apprenticeship, employment and training programs. From 1968 to 1979 he worked with the AFL-CIO's Human Resources Development Institute, becoming executive director in 1975. He has worked extensively to use the resources of organized labor to initiate and operate employment and training programs for veterans, minorities, women, native Americans, and people with handicapping conditions.

PAT CHOATE is senior policy analyst for economics at TRW, Inc., Washington, D.C. He has worked in a variety of management and policy positions in federal and state governments. His research involves management, development, economic policy, and public administration. He received a Ph.D. degree in economics from the University of Oklahoma.

PEDRO GARZA is president of SER-Jobs for Progress, Dallas, Texas. He was previously planning division administrator, deputy director for planning and development, and regional director. Before joining SER in 1972, he was a senior planner for the Economic Opportunities Development Corporation in San Antonio, Texas. He holds an M.A. degree in public affairs from Princeton University and a B.A. degree in government from Texas A&M University.

JAMES M. HOWELL is vice president and chief economist of the First National Bank of Boston, which he joined in 1970. From 1962 to 1970 he held positions in the federal government in the Department of Commerce, in the Federal Reserve System, and as economic adviser to the government of Chile. He has served as trustee or adviser to a number of organizations, including colleges, community groups, employment and training concerns, and economic development activities. He received a Ph.D. degree in economics from Tulane University and a B.A. degree from Texas A&M University.

JANICE MADDEN is associate professor of regional science at the University of Pennsylvania, where she has worked since 1972. Her research has focused on human resources, regional economic development, and the employment of women. She has M.A. and Ph.D. degrees in economics from Duke University and a B.A. from the University of Denver.

PAUL E. PETERSON has just become program director for governmental studies at the Brookings Institution in Washington, D.C. From 1967 to 1983 he was professor of political science and education and also chairman of the Committee on Public Policy Studies at the University of Chicago. His research involves urban politics and policies, especially as they relate to race and education. He holds M.A. and Ph.D. degrees in political science from the University of Chicago and a B.A. degree from Concordia College in Moorhead, Minnesota.

GEORGE R. QUARLES is chief administrator of the Office of Occupational and Career Education in the New York City Board of Education. Previously he served as director of the regional opportunity center program at the City University of New York, director of a manpower training skills center, and teacher of vocational education. He has also taught at Rutgers University, the University of the State of New York, and the New School for Social Research. He has an M.A. degree in vocational education from New York University and a B.S. degree in industrial education from the Hampton Institute.

WILSON C. RILES is now an education consultant in Sacramento, California. From 1971 to 1983 he was superintendent of public instruction, California State Department of Education, where he worked since 1958. He was a teacher and administrator in the Arizona public schools from 1940 to 1954. He holds an M.A. degree in school administration and a B.A. degree in elementary education from Northern Arizona State College.

ISABEL V. SAWHILL is a senior fellow and economist at The Urban Institute in Washington, D.C. Previously she was director of the National Commission for Employment Policy. She has also held positions at the Office of Management and Budget and the U.S. Department of Health, Education, and Welfare and has taught at Goucher College. Her research has focused on employment and training issues and human resources. She holds Ph.D. and B.A. degrees in economics from New York University.

RICHARD F. SCHUBERT became president of the American Red Cross at the beginning of 1983. From 1961 to 1982—except for a five-year leave of absence—he worked for the Bethlehem Steel Corporation in a variety of positions, including president and vice-chairman of the board. From 1970 to 1975 he held various posts in the U.S. Department of Labor, including those of solicitor and under secretary. His career has included work with various universities and community and business organizations. He received an LL.B. degree from the Yale University School of Law and a B.A. degree from Eastern Nazarene College.

FRANCIS T. TUTTLE has been state director of the Oklahoma State Department of Vocational and Technical Education since 1967. Before taking that position, he held various teaching and administrative posts in vocational education in Oklahoma. He has been a consultant for and evaluated vocational education programs in a number of foreign countries. He received an Ed.D. degree in school administration and an M.Ed. from Oklahoma University and a B.S. degree from Oklahoma A&M College.

DAVID A. WISE is Stambaugh Professor of Political Economy at the John F. Kennedy School of Government, Harvard University, where he has taught and conducted research since 1973. His research focuses primarily on youth unemployment—its patterns, explanations, and possible cures. He has a Ph.D. degree in economics from the University of California at Berkeley and a B.A. degree from the University of Washington.

SUSAN W. SHERMAN served as study director of the Committee on Vocational Education and Economic Development in Depressed Areas. Previously she served as study director of the Panel on Testing of Handicapped People and worked with several other committees of the National Research Council. Her principal professional interests include educational and psychological measurement and policy issues in education and the social sciences. She received Ph.D. and M.A. degrees in quantitative psychology from the University of North Carolina at Chapel Hill and an A.B. degree in psychology from Queens College, Charlotte.